BEYOND TREND

BEYOND TREND

HOW TO INNOVATE IN AN OVER-DESIGNED WORLD

MATT MATTUS

Cincinnati, Ohio
www.howdesign.com

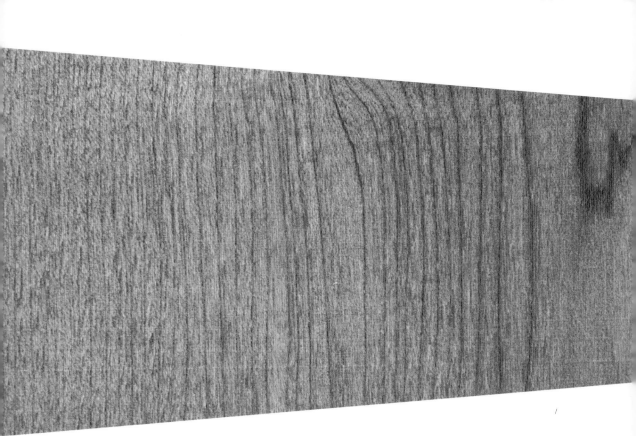

BEYOND TREND. Copyright © 2008 by Matt Mattus. Manufactured in China. All rights reserved. No other part of this book may be reproduced in any form or by any electronic or mechanical means, including information storage and retrieval systems, without permission in writing from the publisher, except by a reviewer, who may quote brief passages in a review. Published by HOW Books, an imprint of F+W Publications, Inc., 4700 East Galbraith Road, Cincinnati, Ohio 45236. (800) 289-0963. First edition.

For more fine books from F+W Publications, visit www.fwpublications.com.

12 11 10 09 08   5 4 3 2 1

Distributed in Canada by Fraser Direct, 100 Armstrong Avenue, Georgetown, Ontario, Canada L7G 5S4, Tel: (905) 877-4411. Distributed in the U.K. and Europe by David & Charles, Brunel House, Newton Abbot, Devon, TQ12 4PU, England, Tel: (+44) 1626 323200, Fax: (+44) 1626 323319, E-mail: postmaster@ davidandcharles.co.uk. Distributed in Australia by Capricorn Link, P.O. Box 704, Windsor, NSW 2756 Australia, Tel: (02) 4577-3555.

Library of Congress Cataloging-in-Publication Data

Mattus, Matt.
  Beyond trend / Matt Mattus.
     p. cm.
  ISBN 978-1-58180-961-9 (hardcover with jacket : alk. paper)
  1. Design, Industrial. 2. Creation (Literary, artistic, etc.) 3. Formalism (Art) I. Title.
  TS171.M386 2008
  745.2--dc22   2008008679

Edited by Amy Schell
Designed by Matt Mattus
Art directed by Grace Ring
Production coordinated by Greg Nock

FOR MY DAD, WHO ENCOURAGED
ME TO COLOR OUTSIDE THE LINES;
AND FOR MY MOM, WHO SAID,
"WHAT LINES?"

ABOUT THE AUTHOR

Working in one of the most trend-oriented industries in the world, for more than twenty years Matt Mattus has led design teams at Hasbro, Inc., in creating break-through branding solutions for kid and teen markets. Matt is on a continuous quest to uncover the influences that inform tomorrow's design. From the obvious to the obscure, he studies culture movements and contemporary trends in art, fashion, architecture, film, food and even rare plants. With a deep respect for pure design excellence, Matt is rarely satisfied with accepting trends at their face value. Instead, he questions and probes phenomena, curious for the real reasons why they occur. With the eye of a designer, the mind of an artist and the knowledge of a historian, Matt doesn't settle for mere connections: he looks for the oxymoronic relationships that exist between truths and trends.

ACKNOWLEDGMENTS

I always knew that books didn't just happen by accident. What I didn't know was the level of collaboration and support it takes to produce one. As with most creative ventures, the process leading up to the idea is as important as the process of executing the idea, and one cannot be more critical than the other. I am so grateful for the many people who believed in my creative ventures.

I first must thank those who encouraged my work as a creative person. Thanks go to Mark Minter, Donna Harkavy, Julie Lohr, Wendy Lessard and Bryn Mooth for opening those bigger doors. All have been portals to greater things.

At HOW Books and F+W Publications, I would like to thank Megan Lane Patrick for her vision, and the resulting opportunity she presented. Thanks for taking a chance with my idea. As a purely visual person, I have a new respect for copyeditors: Thanks to Jeff Suess and Megan Milstead for their skill and patience as they helped craft my mess. I certainly must thank Grace Ring, talented book designer at F+W, for her creative talent and skills. I am so very impressed with her patience and kindness as she made sense out of my InDesign files and improved the look of this book.

Personally, I must thank my friend and colleague, Cheryl McCarthy, who helped separate the big ideas from the useless ones. She was able to make the world's longest Word document into a manuscript.

Mostly, I am especially grateful for having an editor like Amy Schell at HOW Books. I can only imagine what she ever did in a previous life to deserve a first-time author who happens to be a graphic designer, but Amy was able to make me feel that this task was achievable. She coached me through weekly e-mails and phone calls and actually made me feel amazingly capable, even if I missed a few critical deadlines.

Finally, I'd like to thank my partner, Joe Philip, for tolerating my absence for two years as I locked myself in my study. It was Joe's never-fading belief in me that drove me forward in this project and I am forever grateful for his many sacrifices and support.

CONTENTS

INTRODUCTION

"THE WORLD'S MOST NOTEWORTHY CREATIVE LEADERS SHARE CERTAIN TRAITS: THEY ARE INSPIRED BY A CONSTANT DESIRE FOR ORIGINALITY, THEY HAVE A STURDY RESPECT FOR THOSE WITH TRUE TALENT, AND THEY ARE CONSCIOUSLY DRIVEN FORWARD BY A RELENTLESS PURSUIT OF EXCELLENCE." —Matt Mattus

Lately, it's become hard for me to feel satisfied with anything I create.

If I can pinpoint when I started to feel this way, I'd say it was about a year ago on a trip to Cape Cod with my friend Ted. No two people could be more different—something we learned on that trip. Like many creative people, I suffer the burden of an overly curious mind. It never stops. I love to go on vacations that involve hiking in the Alps or trekking for rare orchids in Borneo—or even shopping for cool pottery in Turkey. Vacations which require merely *rest* horrify me. So while the idea of doing nothing for a week and lying on the beach was exciting for Ted, I was nearly hyperventilating about the creative restrictions such isolation brought. I only offered to join him because he was my best friend, and he was looking for someone to split costs. Besides, he convinced me that a break would be good for me. But I soon learned that our preference for opposite vacation styles was not the biggest difference between Ted and me.

Ted is a hardworking, confidently practical, proud-to-embrace-his-blue-collar-roots sort of guy. He also views the world through the eyes

opposite page >> A screen print by artist Steven Harrington of Pasadena, California.

of a realist. I, on the other hand, view the world as a creative person: hardly a realist, more of an opportunist. Like a hunter and gatherer, I constantly look for stimuli, for prey.

One night, as we were shopping on Commercial Street in Provincetown, Ted pointed out how many people were wearing cargo shorts and sloppy, torn, vintage T-shirts. Ted is all about anti-fashion. If his jeans were from Wal-Mart, he'd say, "So what—that's where they came from."

I started pointing out that many of the cargo shorts that he was seeing actually evolved from a collegiate recycling of Carhartt branded painter pants and work clothes. This made him angry. He said, "Fashion is really all bullshit. It brainwashes mindless people to think that they need something. It's all so meaningless and wasteful."

I began to tease him that those brown Carhartt jeans that his buddies and family are touting as anti-establishment are very cool—even trendy—with the skater culture in Germany.

He snapped back. "Why do all of you elitist designers need to ruin everything for us real people who earned the right—as hardwork-

تذوق طعم أحلام اليقظة
aste the daydream.

STARBUCKS COFFEE

ممزوجة بالقهـ
ended Coffee

rich traditional flavour
e blended with premium
ee will take you away.

جافا تشيب
فـــراپتشيــنـو
ممزوجة بالقهوة

JAVA CHIP

ing plumbers and carpenters or construction workers—to wear these clothes that are like tools to us? Now, all of you affected fashionistas are ruining it for all of us who don't give a damn about what's in or out."

Ouch. Maybe he needed this vacation. But then he said something that really caught my attention.

"Why can't people just be more honest? I mean, I think everyone should just be happy with the basics: blue jeans and a T-shirt. Then we can judge each other on the same plane, against what really matters. I am completely

p.2 >> *Left:* Wendy's restaurant in Ebisu, Japan. *Right:* Nighttime view of the fountains at the Bellagio Hotel, Las Vegas, Nevada.
p.3 >> A Starbucks in Riyadh, Saudi Arabia.

p.4 >> *Left:* Hollywood may portray the pyramids at Giza as if they are in the middle of a desert, but people can also enjoy them while munching on a bucket of chicken at KFC and looking out the window. *Right:* We may ask for more originality, but at the same time, we expect branded luxury. Cunard Cruise Line's new *Queen Mary 2* surely raises the bar on design and experience, but with such masstige

happy with my basic Levi's and a nice simple white Hanes T-Shirt."

Totally unaffected by design. Rrrright.

We all can learn something from this. Design has become so powerful that it is entering the danger zone. The real facts are that design can give a generation a presumption of moral superiority. This, in turn, can link to such contentious issues as race or gender or class.

Design has become very attainable, very personal and very public. Now, every choice we make is tracked. We also are smarter, and superficially, we know that we can use design to communicate certain messages. I'm affected, you're affected, even Ted is affected by design. We are now in a blurred, over-designed world.

After our vacation, Ted moved on to believe in what he believes in, and I came to the blunt realization that not everyone sees life through a designer's eye. Many people are blind to design. They don't see how it informs our lives, how it drives us to new ideas, new attitudes, and new insights, how it empowers us all. Design has real value.

luxuries as a Canyon Ranch SpaClub and a Todd English restaurant, the authenticity level drifts dangerously close to the Las Vegas strip. **p.5 >>** *Right:* Design can mean creature comforts. Traveling dogs and cats receive a complimentary gift pack on the new Cunard *Queen Mary 2*. With kennels and adjacent indoor and outdoor walking areas, passengers can now share their luxury experience with their pets.

Or does it?

Our discussion stayed with me for a long time. It turned out to be the catalyst for many hours of personal reflection and, ultimately, it led to this book. I began to question my own behavior and beliefs. Was I really over-affected by trends, and did this make me a shallow person? Were my accomplishments in design truly not achievements? Was I just a pawn in a totalitarian, material world? Or was Ted's position on design and brands simply coming from fear? And if so, where was that fear coming from?

I started to question the human gift that creates sensual experience—not sexual, but sensual—the experience of our senses. Think about your favorite color, or flavor, or smell. They are your favorites because your experiences with them have been pleasing to your senses, and they have presumably become familiar as you repeatedly experience them. Familiarity is constructed through experience. But, does sticking to the familiar mean that we have become too lazy to experience anything new? Or is there nothing new anymore?

p.6, p.7 >> Brilliant orange squares line the walkways of New York City's Central Park in this NASA IKONOS image. Taken on February 12, 2005, the image marks the opening day of The Gates art exhibit by Christo and Jeanne-Claude, which featured 7,500 gates draped with saffron-colored fabric.

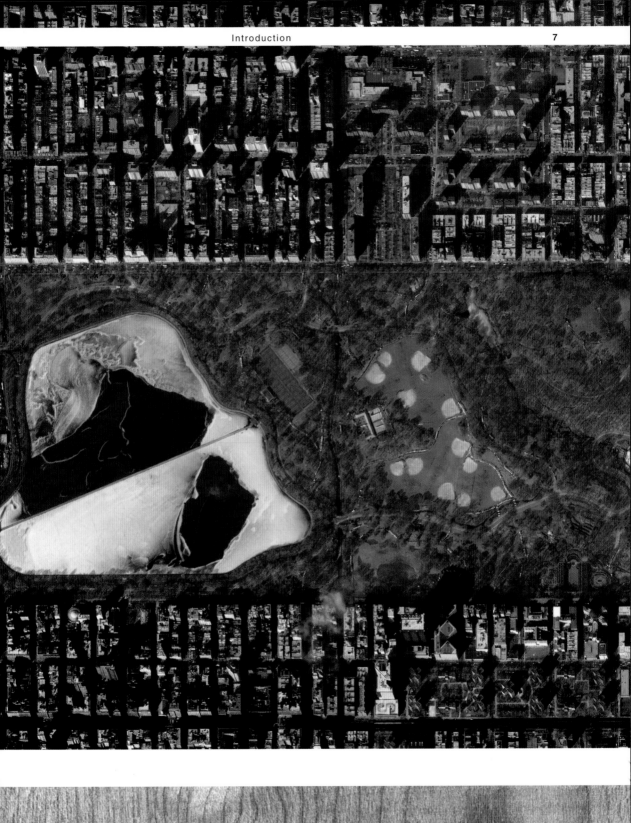

IS THERE ANYTHING NEW?

When was the last time you experienced something truly new? If you're a designer, what was the last new color combination that blew you away? If you're a fashion designer, what was the last truly revolutionary new style you found? If you're a painter, when were you last so affected by a work of art that it moved you to a new aesthetic?

As a designer myself, I fear the possibility that we may be reaching a point where there is nothing new to discover. Experiencing new ideas and sights is a fundamental joy to many of us who seek more than the familiar. The notion that we are merely repeating ideas that others have already expressed greatly disturbs me, since it appears that cultural development has hit either an apex or a brick wall. Neither development is good news.

Design and invention are two characteristics that help define our species. The ability to discover—either through curiosity or experimentation—has enabled mankind to overcome fear through experience, and to create a world rich with structure and art. We build tools, we migrate and we make

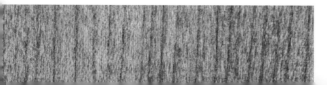

p.8 >> Dan Goodsell, coauthor of *Krazy Kids' Food*, collects art from the latter part of the twentieth century, including this Ray Patin frame from an early 1960s animated television commercial

improvements. We have harnessed creativity. We have taken the basic requirements for life—shelter, food, and clothing—and, as humans, we've applied creative design … and then more design … and more … until today there is nothing that hasn't been "designed." We have put our stamp on just about everything, from how we live to what we eat and what we feel. This may be a dream state for those of us who are aesthetically inclined. Others of us must ask, is all of this necessary? Good? Right? Important? Or even useful?

And all this "designed lifestyle" is happening against a backdrop of conflicting needs and desires. On one hand, we desire environmentally conscious products, yet we stuff ourselves with fast food. Gourmet cuisine has morphed into a fusion of unlikely and sometimes inedible options. Designer labels are "must-haves," yet the ten-dollar T-shirt at Wal-Mart is equally a necessity. In short, we want it all, in no linear order. So, as designers, how do we cope? What fleeting expectation are we meant to contend with today?

for Jell-O. **p.9 >>** *Reddening*, a photograph by Laura S. Kicey. One formula of shampoo or toothpaste might have worked in the past, but today's consumer is desperately seeking experience. As brands struggle to shift strategy, design has to keep up the appeal.

TOO MUCH DESIGN

Design has become an addiction. And just like any addiction, the more we have, the more we want. As we train ourselves to demand more, we risk becoming numb with abundance. Is color infinite? Are combinations of styles endless? How long before we start repeating them? Or are we already there?

We have more access to information than ever before. It's mind-boggling how much we can know, and how quickly we can learn it. Very little information is hidden today. The term "information overload" would have little meaning to your grandparents, who were informed by the morning newspaper and the six o'clock news on just three local stations. Our super-busy world of the Internet and thousands of television stations over-inform us with an abundance of nothing. Yet, we are still not satisfied. Like addicts, we need more. This over-abundance is exacerbated by the growing problem of having too many choices. We have a thousand television channels and still there is nothing to watch.

And it doesn't end with design or entertainment. Even something as primal as eating

p.10 >> View of the moon rising over earth. Image courtesy of the Image Science and Analysis Laboratory, NASA-Johnson Space Center.

has progressed (or is it regressed?) to a point where our choices are based on values other than need: whether it's how natural a product is, how it speaks to our desire for a new taste, or if it has a new package design. We have figured out that what we eat communicates something about us, about our status or our moral position, about whether we're green or processed or worldly. We are as likely to choose a product based on what it says about us as we are to choose it for the experience it brings us. This mode of consuming effects where we go on vacation, what we buy our kids and what brand of fast food we eat. Have you looked at the toothbrush aisle at your local supermarket lately? How many colors of gum-massaging brushes do we need? Procter & Gamble's Head & Shoulders dandruff shampoo used to come as one, single formula—it now comes in twelve expressions.

Desire, choice, abundance: it all adds up to design. Design is the process that considers what a product can and should deliver, crafts it into a neat little package that expresses meaning, and makes a personal connection to an individual. Sounds a little bit like art, doesn't it?

THE ART OF DESIGN

Inventing new ideas requires tracking trends, but we must be careful not to confuse tracking with following. Innovation does not come through following. It comes from being informed. Creatives must use trends as information, not as checklists. You must understand where they are coming from, what is influencing them; and then look beyond them for new threads, the new influences that might possibly connect to become a trend. This is Beyond Trend thinking, a practice which involves collecting as much

p.12, p.13 >> Stills from a video created for retailer Target entitled "Revolutions." This was designed to appeal in large format when displayed in Times Square, New York City, celebrating the opening of the first NYC Target store. Designed by Catalyst Studios, Minneapolis. **p.13 >>** *Bottom right:* Television spot for McCann Worldgroup's Microsoft Windows campaign for the Microsoft XP

launch in the Australian market. The spot demonstrates how agencies and design firms collaborate across the planet as they create and design. Design and animation by Stardust Studios, a creative production company.

information as you can consume, and then evaluating it against what you already know.

Innovation means "new," and anything valued as "new" has become the standard for measuring innovation, especially the marketing of products. As trends peak in our over-populated world of sameness, it's the new innovations—the ones that have been fortified with real influence and original meaning—that bring the most potential. The current business language which includes terms like "storytelling" and "experiential design" is firm proof that "meaning" has been identified as a valuable

asset in products. There is little room for the old-school 1980s marketing of following patterns and mimicking the competition. In the new world of beyond-trend consumers, a double-bladed razor will quickly be out-marketed by a quad-blade razor. But the real market-breaker will be the first business to introduce the item that redefines a category: The dream today is to invent the item that makes all the other razors obsolete. Why shave if you have the iRazor?

Difference gets noticed. Innovation destroys the competition. Winning through design is no longer pretty, it's become brutally rough.

p.14 >> inNEWvation, a logo created by the author for a Hasbro innovation summit. **p.15 >>** The cover of a report, created by the author for Hasbro, on visual trends in London.

But the idea of "meaning" is hardly new to most conscious creators, since meaning is the heart of any real, honest creation from thoughtful artists and designers. Imagine art without meaning. Museums are full of influential paintings that are dismissed by the general population as "modern art" simply because people don't connect with them. A connection requires that the viewer does research, becomes informed about the work, and understands the influence as well as the cultural impact of that particular piece. But who has the time or desire to invest all that work when you have kids to drive to soccer practice and dinner to get on the table?

The reality is that most people don't give a hoot about such things as "culturally important" design and art, or its meaning. You've probably heard comments like, "Art is something that only the rich can appreciate," or "Art and design don't mean anything in a world where people are starving and nations are at war." But there is also a personal aspect to art and design. In a world of repeats, reruns and recycling, a personal connection to art is valuable to both you as the designer or artist and the viewer. And in the world of design, which is really about business, the personal connection translates into influence—exactly what the business

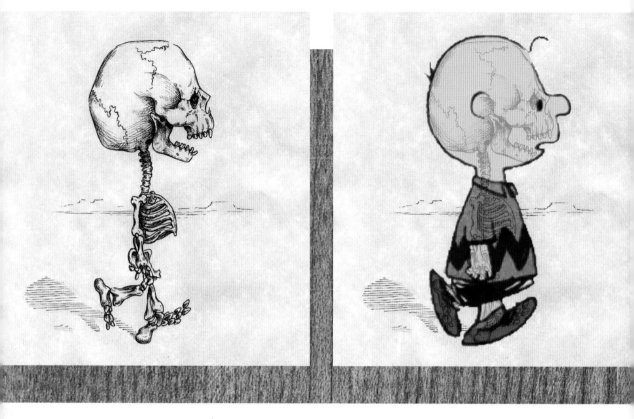

(whom you are designing for) wants. How the design achieves that personal connection is through finding what the people want: individuality and meaning. In other words, art.

THE POWER TO CHANGE

So, as designers, we see the world in a different way. We can continue to nurture our gift of design, and answer the call to create and invent new things. We may never be understood by the non-creatives, or be respected as a surgeon is, or be able to explain to our own parents what we do, but the ultimate calling of a creative designer is as important and necessary now as ever before. Is it hard? Sure. That deep-seated and often deeply secret desire to start a firestorm in a world where seemingly every design trend is in play all at once—what's harder than that? But what could be more exciting?

Power is in the hands of the creative, the power to change lives with a single image—a photo, drawing, concept, structure, vehicle, aircraft, garment or anything else that the creative mind can invent. Remember that design itself may be as simple as art, but it also can be defined as the ultimate human expression.

p.16 >> Charlie, part of the Skeletal Systems character studies by artist and illustrator Michael Paulus of Portland, Oregon.
p.17 >> Designs by Andrew Groves of IMAKETHINGS, for Foundation Skateboards' "Secret Beast" Pro Series.

We must not trivialize design, for it comes from our human brains. Design is important and is critical to the advancement of our species. The responsibility that comes with this very human gift to create is enormous, for design can also destroy us. Conscious creation is a core responsibility all designers must practice, and it doesn't matter if you are designing a heat-seeking missile, a high-functioning hospital bed, or a mold for Gummy Bears. Design has the potential to change attitudes and the power to change culture in a single gesture.

This book is about power.

>>> *CHAPTER*

THE END OF
TREND

For the past twenty years, I have held a number of creative positions at Hasbro, the toy giant and maker of Transformers, G.I. Joe, My Little Pony, Monopoly, Scrabble, Trivial Pursuit, Playskool, and Mr. Potato Head, to name a few—basically, most of the classic toys and games we all grew up with. My career path was pretty typical: I matured from packaging designer to design manager to creative director, until I moved into a new group formed to take on the larger challenges of Hasbro's emerging entertainment and IP development.

IP stands for "intellectual property," a term typically associated with lawyers and gray suits, but which has more recently taken on a larger, creative definition. Today, behind the doors of the world's most competitive businesses, IP is quietly becoming a new way to speak about brand development. It combines the ideas of meaning, story and creativity to go further than the original expression of a brand into more surprising and effective experiences. Marketers might call it EQ (emotional quotient). They might say it's the story of the brand, the meaning of the brand or the brand essence. But whatever you call

p.19 >> *Left:* Optimus Prime, a character from Hasbro's Transformers brand. *Right, from top to bottom:* Transformers movie poster. Design concept for tween girl fashion magazine designed by the author. Blythe doll licensing guide, designed by the author. Megatron, another Transformers robot. Special effects still from the Dreamworks feature film *Transformers.*

TIBET   YEMEN   SHANGHAI

it, it explains today's explosion of brands in unexpected places.

It's why a World of Coca-Cola store doesn't seem out of place in Las Vegas. It's why Dove's Campaign for Real Beauty reduces women to tears. It's why it makes sense to take a trip to outer space on Virgin Galactic. And why the *Transformers* movie was a project that Steven Spielberg and Michael Bay were anxious to take on.

Through the lens of brand expansion into storytelling and entertainment, my view of the role of creatives in the business envi-

ronment was forever changed. It was clear where the role of visual arts in business was inevitably going. It would no longer be enough to simply communicate with the consumer. Now, our job would be to move the end-user emotionally, in the deepest possible way. So I set out to discover how others were doing this … to see what I could learn from marketing powerhouses and young upstarts alike.

In 2003, I moved into a role we titled Director of Visual Trends. I informed designers of emerging trends that I gathered from travel-

p.20 >> *Left:* It seems that there is no escaping the branding of the world. Here, Tibetan wine is marketed in western China and Tibet. *Center:* The Pepsi generation's graphics translate well even deep in the Republic of Yemen. *Right:* If you think a Starbucks on every corner completes the American experience, try Shanghai, China, or even Milan. As global brands grow, so does world sameness.

SHANGHAI   ISTANBUL   HONG KONG

ing to known trend centers, as well as some obscure ones. I dug into this role with gusto, planned my first trend-hunting trip to all of the major taste-making centers in the world, and set off to chart the course of the future for my company. From Tokyo to Milan, Los Angeles to London, I explored whatever I could find—in alleys, galleries and boutique shops. I dutifully captured my findings with my digital camera, knowing that I'd come back to the office triumphant and inspiring every designer in the company with a global view of the big and small-but-soon-to-be-big influencers around the world. I could see

the PowerPoint presentation in my head as I boarded the plane.

But by the third leg of the trip, the PowerPoint deck was not quite so clear in my mind any longer. In fact, I was starting to get scared that everyone would think I'd been on a whirlwind, worldwide boondoggle. I was seeing what other creatives were also just starting to uncover … and it wasn't pretty.

It wasn't even ugly.

It was nothing.

p.21 >> *Left:* Chinese workers practice Tai Chi in front of posters for Disney's *The Lion King*, in Shanghai, China. *Center:* Even if you flunked your last Turkish language class, you will hardly die of thirst in Istanbul. *Right:* In 2007, fans around the planet shared their excitement surrounding the premiere of *Transformers*. Here, a poster adds to the excitement in Hong Kong.

RIYADH

Global Sameness

Around the world, nothing much was new. Oh sure, there was mid-century modernism, and craft, and the green movement—all microtrends I had already identified through my daily Internet research back at the office. But really, that wasn't what I was looking for since I already knew those influences were starting to mix. What surprised me first was that besides the obvious cultural differences in Japan or England, there was really very little new beyond the mid-century modern expressions that emerged back then. What

unique designs I did see were apparently not adopted, as they often appeared only in specialty boutiques and one-off artist shops. Besides, those designs all contradicted each other, so they couldn't be considered the next hot trend.

And, to top things off, I couldn't really offer anything new to answer the question executives always ask me. And you know the question. It sounds something like this: "The seventies are big right now. Can you show me what the next hot look will be? Will it be the eighties?" I knew people back at the office

p.22 >> Brand identity can be expressed simply in form (and two colors). The IKEA experience still delivers to consumers in Riyadh, Saudi Arabia. **p.23 >>** *Top left:* A *Star Wars* Stormtrooper guards over London's Trafalgar Square during a promotion for the film's debut. Photo by Bryan Allison. *Top right:* Subway sandwich shop in Dubai. *Bottom:* A Gap store in Tokyo's youth-trendy Harajuku section.

LONDON

TOKYO

DUBAI

AUSTRIA

were expecting to hear big trend headlines. All I was finding was yesterday's news.

With that, I realized a larger and more important trend in design: that true, innovative work was being done by few and noticed by even fewer; that those who could break frame were relegated to the side streets and back alleys of culture. This gigantic influence of big business on our culture today was, in fact, arresting the very culture it was trying to market to. That phrases like "global efficiencies" could actually be culture killers. Business isn't interested in moving the human experience forward but,

instead, moving the bottom line forward, and bottom lines *love* efficiency.

The truth is, it was so obvious that I never considered it. We are now visually globalized. Business became global, the Internet became global, so why didn't I imagine that design trends would become global? Not global by being available to the entire world, but global by the fact that they have been integrated, blurred, consumed and digested. Design trends had been affected by all cultures—not just one—and were ultimately transformed into a murky, singular sea of a reinterpreted

p.24 >> *Top:* MPreis is redefining the food shopping experience in the Tyrolean Alps.The progressive Austrian food market chain challenges various architects to make grocery shopping more of an experience than a chore. *Bottom:* Cappellini lamp by designer Marcel Wanders at the Milan Furniture Fair. **p.25 >>** Furniture collection called "Dream" by Marcel Wanders at the Milan Furniture Fair.

mid-century-modern sameness. It was still all stunning and beautiful design, but I couldn't imagine what could be next.

You have probably noticed that it is becoming increasingly difficult to tell a Target TV ad from a Sears ad. Once unique Starbucks interiors with their artist-created murals and comfortable atmosphere of Italian lamps and lounge chairs now look like every other fast food bistro, from Panera Bread to Boston Market. Clothing retailers like J.Crew, Gap, Banana Republic and Brooks Brothers all sell similar merchandise—chinos and khakis and polo shirts. The democratization of design is quickly becoming the homogenization of design. What's worse is that these restaurants and retailers are found all over the world, and they all carry the same merchandise at the same time. A Gap in Tokyo has the same black T-shirt for sale as the Gap in Paramus, New Jersey. If this is what the goal of the democratization of design was, then I don't want it.

What does all this have to do with designers? "This ubiquitous-ness of design," as *The New Yorker* architectural critic Paul Goldberger puts it, "is making us, in a sense, numbed by

p.26 >> Catalyst Studios' Target animation for Times Square brings the Target experience to life, thirty stories high. **p.27 >>** Brazilian illustrator Adhemas Batista's work for South American mobile phone giant Claro modernizes collage and helps it resonate with the youthful consumer the brand intends to reach.

too much design around us, by the sense that it is all too familiar, and that we need what are, in effect, higher and higher levels of design intensity to respond." Sounds a little too much like design addiction to me, but the point is sound, especially if you are a designer in a business that demands excellence and future thinking on your part. In an over-designed world, how does a designer design?

TECHNOLOGY AFFECTS DESIGN

Technology has become a complicating factor to the challenge of design in several ways.

Not only has it brought about new tools and software, easier connections, and the digital age—see "The Digital Boomer Effect" on page 135—it has made design accessible to the masses.

Take shopping, for instance. Consumers are under tighter scrutiny than ever before, as technology allows the industry to track, measure and calculate every single purchase a consumer makes. Manufacturers can instantly gather statistics on how many of those Michael Graves teapots have sold in every Target store in America, so that as soon as one moves

p.28 >> A colorful and stylized composition by Adhemas Batista, created for the Sensorama Exhibition in Berlin, Germany. **p.29** >> Australian firm Elenberg Fraser reinvents the idea of "ski lodge." This award-winning firm designed a world-class apartment hotel that brings the city to the slopes. This pink, lavender and chrome playset for the rich is located at Mt. Buller ski resort, a three hour drive from Melbourne.

through the register, a manufacturing plant (most likely in China) has that exact piece of data on its screen. Inventory is managed down to every individual Band-Aid box.

This information influences not only how many to stock on the shelves, but who is buying what, where they are buying it, and how many are sold. In short, it tracks the trends. That might be too much information, though. It's all data, no influence. If everything is popular, there is no way to decipher actual trends. Today, the rhythm of design has been upended by so many converging and contra-dictory influences that the days of trend are numbered. Count 'em ...

Another effect is that the advances in computer technology now allow pretty much anyone to design. What at one time required typesetters, type and copy fitters, copywriters, concept designers, layout designers, mechanical artists, photo art directors, print quality controllers and printer approvals with film separators can now be achieved by one person sitting behind a desk with a computer ... and the marketing person standing over her shoulder saying, "Green doesn't sell. Make it blue."

p.30 >> *Left:* The power of design is best demonstrated by the principles behind Martha Stewart, Martha Stewart Living and MSLO brands. Martha Stewart is actually less of a domestic diva and more of an ambassador to design excellence. *Right:* A Home Depot store, North America's answer to do-it-yourself home repair. **p.31 >>** A Michaels craft store aisle.

The availability of technology doesn't automatically transform someone into a designer. It's not as simple as walking into an Apple Store and buying a software program on design. The tools of design available today are awesome, and may make it easier and more accessible for most anyone to attempt true design creation, but a certain amount of talent, skill, and education must also be present. Design is a practice, but today it has also become a pastime and a hobby. There is nothing wrong with design as a hobby; in fact, I fully endorse it as a mind-growing exercise, but there is a risk emerging in our field, because there is

no such thing as a licensed graphic designer. The future of artistic design may be headed towards a messy collision until some parameters are established.

Do-It-Yourself Design

One threat to the future of visual design is the do-it-yourselfers. It's Saturday morning at the Home Depot, and a crowd builds around the paint chip aisle. Eager homemakers, swatches in hand, match tints of sage green and butter yellow to cushions and upholstery. Professional designers and colorists shriek

as these homemade creatives select paint chips as if their living rooms were lit with the same florescent lights as the store. They are in desperate need of design intervention. The entire system supports them, too, with companies like Disney, Ralph Lauren and Martha Stewart having licensed paint lines. Television programs pitch designer against designer, and make designing one's bedroom a reality show. DIY (do it yourself) is even a cable television network. Is this simply self-expression? Or is it a, "It's fun to design!" sort of play experience? Or, is it a new movement of do-it-yourself-so-you-don't-have-to-hire-a-

designer-to-do-it? (A quick note on crafts: Craft stores such as Michaels and Jo-Ann are in every town in America. From scrapbooking to quilt-making, these craft cultures are not really about design at all. They are more about self-expression than design. They use established designs, then assemble and customize them. This is design by template. It's fun and safe. There is no threat to designers.)

Today, anyone can declare himself creative. Creativity is no longer exclusive to the creative class, but is encouraged in everyone. Proof of design's new validation in business

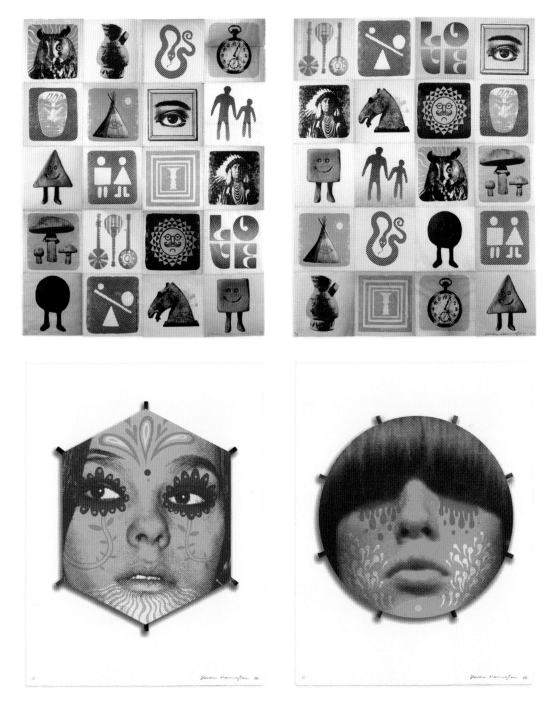

p.32 >> Snap Wrap wrapping paper by Catalyst Studios of Minneapolis, Minnesota. **p.33 >>** Silk screen illustrations by Pasadena, California, artist Steven Harrington, © 2008.

p.34 >> Silk screen illustrations by Pasadena artist Steven Harrington, © 2008. **p.35 >>** Illustration for "The Coke Side of Life" campaign by Non-Format.

is the fact that the most respected business schools are opening design programs. Stanford, the consummate "B" school, has now opened a "D" school. Leading business publications, such as the *Harvard Business Review* and *BusinessWeek*, have featured design as one of the last platforms on which to compete. As the value of design rises to the top, expect greater competition and greater definition between those who are capable and those who are less. Gifted designers with the skill to assemble breakthrough ideas will have to work harder to rise above the crowds of linear-thinkers who are more concerned about the process of design than the visual aspect.

The rise of individualized design affects the design community in both positive and negative ways. The positive effect, of course, is that we need more designers—especially good ones. It has resulted in new recognition and awareness of the value of good design. But now anyone can declare himself a designer, which trivializes a career in design. This poses a serious challenge for anyone seeking creative talent, but who might not be qualified to evaluate it (see

"Making Changes to a Creative Organization" on page 148).

However, there will still be opportunities for those who have the skills and talent to produce quality design. Even though anyone can explore his creative side through Apple's iLife software or the Martha Stewart Living Omnimedia web site by clicking and dragging images onto templates, someone still has to design those templates. That someone is the real designer.

Someone with extraordinary talent who can create pure newness in a world of sameness will rise to the top. Creative excellence will draw a deep and impenetrable line between those who play with design and those with the rare talent to create magic.

p.36, p.37 >> Non-Format's 2006 exhibition Make A Fuss at Vallery, Barcelona, Spain. **p.37** >> *Center:* Music packaging for Anoice Remmings, Important Records. *Bottom:* Carhartt might mean wholesome work wear in America, but the brand also has become successful as an alternative expression to urban street culture in many parts of Northern Europe. Budapest designer Karoly Kiralyfalvi is one of

many artists hired by the brand to customize their stores, each one unique and irresistable to the skaters, skallies and fashionistas who are hungry for an alternative statement of authenticity.

DESIGN ADDICTION

BIG BUSINESS DISCOVERS THE VALUE OF DESIGN

Designers and creative professionals have never been in such high demand as they are now. Historically, value has always driven the development of culture and design, so imagine what value such originality has in our world of mass-produced products?

Think about it. What would a business pay for something so completely new and original, an invention so different, so disruptive to conventional thinking yet so "must-have," that it would make the iPhone seem virtually Victorian? What would that be worth? The answer is: a lot.

A sign that the game has changed is that the big business schools are opening design campuses, and that talent recruiters are not just waiting for resumes to come across their desks, but companies like Martha Stewart Living Omnimedia and Disney are recruiting right at the design schools before graduates even start their senior year. Internships at the most creative corporations are as competitive as medical residencies at the world's best hospitals.

Design is undeniably hot in today's business world. The only thing is, what comes next?

TREND
ENDER »

2

MORE IS MORE

CAN WE DEAL WITH LESS?

Less isn't necessarily more. Take TV channels, for instance. We all want more. But more channels don't really offer anything new, and we're stuck with the same old, same old—just more of it.

So, today we are supposed to be more educated than our grandparents, right? But why do we want more of everything? We demand to be more informed, healthier and more global. We are more involved, more emotionally in-touch, more responsible and even more comfortable with ourselves (or at least more medicated) than any other generation before.

So, if our generation is so smart, why are we so blind when it comes to the future and ultimate possibility that more just may lead to less? And how are we prepared to deal with less when we expect so much more?

Business trends also demand more. More competitive, more meaningful, more responsible and more sustainable. Oh, right—and more profitable. But one hears little about the abundance of visual culture. More devices, more images, more messages and more design. This is a time when less feels old, and in a strange way, even less feels like more.

FEAR

FEAR AND THE ABUSE OF ORIGINAL THOUGHT

Designers have favorites. A secret Indian restaurant, a special source for fabric or paper, a unique cupcake bakery, a certain breed of dog or a fifteen-year-old T-shirt you just can't part with.

The creative craves the sensation of seeing or buying or experiencing something new for the first time, yet for others, the unfamiliar is not appealing. We all know people who are afraid of things that are new. The reasons are many. It may be a brand that your mother never bought, or a style that you never felt comfortable with. We humans are trained to like what we are taught, often by our parents or the people who raised us. We measure what we adopt against our innate sense of

desire and fear, whether we are conscious of it or not.

Designers are a little different. The more creative an individual is, the more "dangerous" they often are. It might be motorcycles and drugs, or it may be fearless travel and extreme confidence with testing new color choices.

As designers, we must understand how our audience approaches something new to help them overcome those uncomfortable feelings. We must set the bait to pull the audience through the realm of "something new" without letting them off the hook. It's the age-old quandary of originality.

Now, set that against the current climate of design, where mass market is literally on the heels of boutique originality, where any nascent design movement races straight to public proliferation without a chance to nurture itself into a fully-realized, complex influence. Instead, originality is immediately knocked off by the biggest retailers, who are the hungriest for something new. The design industry is being short-circuited by the race for something new, while its audience is breathlessly trying not to be scared out of their fifteen-dollar gauchos. In short, design is eating its young.

TREND
ENDER >>
4

RECYCLING

WHAT DESIGN MOVEMENT ARE WE IN AGAIN?

So, here we are in the twenty-first century, and I never thought that we would still be buying mid-century-inspired furniture. And where are the jet packs? Our world is recycling trends at a rate reaching warp speed: where once the fifties and sixties were fair game, it seems as if we are discoing through the seventies as long as we can drag it out, and whatever visual icons we can squeeze out of the horrid eighties and meaningless nineties are being used up rapidly. Shouldn't the design community be freaking out about what's next instead of cycling back to mid-century modern again in a desperate mode of post-post-recycling?

Since we have been in this never-ending cycle of recycling since the mid 1980s, we also have been educating a whole new generation who see the older movements with different eyes. It's why a forty-year-old cringes at bell-bottoms and hip-huggers, and a teen demands boot-cut lowriders or gauchos. The design world has blurred the meaning of trends, as well as destroyed any relatively recent design movement in the process.

What about the seasonal phenomenon of trends? Business is scared stiff at the thought of no apparent design movement or that there might not be a new look for the back-to-school season. The same thing that is happening to television news is happening to design—it's becoming sensationalized, and yet there is nothing to say anymore.

News flash: The 1990s are back … now what?

TREND
ENDER >>

5

CONTRADICTION

THE EXISTENCE OF CONFLICTING TRENDS

If you are not confused yet, you will be. Call it beautiful, fun, or busy, but today's contradiction in style may also be a warning sign that culturally, we might be running out of new visual ideas. As designers search the world for anything that can inspire them, they are using up inspiration faster and faster. Trends behave very much like wildfire, and our creative forests risk running out of trees. Sure, great things also come in our visually saturated world, but we creatives should also be mindful about what we wish for. In a world where the biggest retailers tout that "design is for everyone," creatives in charge of delivering such hopefulness are finding that real innovation is more and more difficult to obtain.

Which begs the question that many of us are afraid to ask: Is invention a limited resource?

Today, as the world's most talented designers juxtapose contradicting styles in an effort to achieve exciting designs, you can't help but ask what might be next. Such looks may feel new and fresh, but looking forward, how many new combinations of influence can actually occur before visual deficiency begins? Some bigger questions might be, "Is our culture approaching a point of global creative saturation?" Or on a more positive note, "Will this trend of surprising and unpredictable juxtaposition lead to something even newer, something that we have not even imagined yet?"

If contradiction is what everyone is doing, could it be our last visual trend?

TREND
ENDER >>

6

VISUAL EXHAUSTION

OK, NOW I'M NUMB

What excites you? When was the last time you saw something new—something you had never seen before? I don't know about you, but I'm getting a little bored now.

Becoming culturally stagnant has happened before, but the opposite has also happened—periods of high cultural development which anthropologists call "cultural florescences." Respected socio-anthropologist A. L. Kroeber cites a correlation between intellectual advancements and aesthetic leaps in his 1945 book, *Configurations of Culture Growth*. One can see clearly what Kroeber identified simply by looking at a timeline of the past five hundred years. One can see how such game-changers as Darwin, Einstein and advancements in design and art changed social and cultural comprehension. Such cultural florescences are rare enough—three or four perhaps, ever. The nearest to today was in the late 1800s when the industrial revolution allowed new opportunities for world travel, electricity and modernism.

More concerning to us should be what happens when cultures peak. Both ancient Greece and ancient Rome are cited in Kroeber's book as examples of cultural florecences that ran out of ideas and became stagnant. Applying his theory on why cultures collapse paints a frightening theoretical picture of our future.

Yet, I feel positive about today because we know so much more than his generation could ever have predicted. Most impactful is that we are so globally connected, that the definition of culture as undefined by national boundaries has changed everything. Any peaks in visual culture need to be measured on a global scale, not a national one.

For designers, any of these theories present unprecedented new challenges … a world that craves familiar sameness, yet is moving toward the unfamiliar.

RANDOM INFLUENCE

DESIGNERS WORK HARDER TO GET OUR ATTENTION

Thoughtful influence that appears random is not easy. Successful creative solutions that demonstrate this best are executed by the most artistic of creatives. The danger is that once culture accepts random influence as a model, it is hard to move forward. Behaving very much like shock art in the sixties, such ideas as juxtaposition and contradiction can only catch the attention of the consumer for a moment. A greater danger is the practice of amateur designers practicing random influence use.

Knowing what to use as influence, and when to use it, is not something that can be learned.

Much like cooking, there are plenty of recipes out there, but original thinking is best left to the learned. Experimentation can lead to great discoveries, but only a small population will ever achieve originality. The difference with design today is that taste has become more subjective, and the materials for use (or misuse) are everywhere.

Influence is not a trend-ender; it's a trend starter. Random is the death of influence.

Be deliberate.

SELF EXPRESSIONISM

COULD THIS TREND BE OUR
LAST CREATIVE MOVEMENT?

Our visual abundance isn't just becoming boring; it's becoming addictive and controlling. In many ways, the "more" movement is leading design around by the nose. Today's generation exists in such a confusing world of mixed visual messages that we are on the verge of a state of visual chaos. We believe this abundance of visual culture allows us to define ourselves down to within an inch of our true selves. But, to be honest, chaos is really only describing our mood of the moment, a mood that we have little control over unless we can find meaning in it.

True design must be of the moment and last well past it. Design is meant to exist on a continuum of all sorts of meaning, one that reaches from ephemeral to permanent, entertaining to life changing. If design can elevate us emotionally, what is happening today in our visual world of chaotic contrast and multiplicity on demand? Can design still captivate?

True design may be chaos, but only if that chaos is tempered with a deliberate, visionary intent to move us emotionally. Our current trend of meaningful design-for-everyone may just lead us to a euphoric high, but the more important journey may be what comes after the high, when the novelty wears off.

Our current fascination with craft and self-expression with the rise of Michaels craft stores, Martha Stewart Living, and do-it-yourself programming and magazines more than hint at the deep desire for finding more meaning in our visual and virtual lives.

MEANING

FINDING MEANING IN BRANDS

Does everything have to have meaning? Do you remember the first time that you heard the term "meaning" when asked to create something? How about this newer idea of "adding story"? You may think that this whole "story" and "meaning" thing is nothing more than some fluffy, MBA textbook concept that the new marketing manager from Yale is trying to use to impress her boss, but you're wrong. In fact, meaning and story are two new business concepts that affect design more than any business trends that have occurred in the past one hundred years. The problem is that along with this power to connect comes responsibility not to abuse this complex relationship.

In order for something to have meaning, it must connect emotionally with the consumer. Unfortunately, one of the easiest ways to connect is to remind the consumer of the past. No wonder our visual world is overflowing with terms like "vintage," "retro," "antique," "vault," and "classic"; not only is it easy, it might be all that is left. Marketing today is in the same quandary as design, and as marketers strive to behave more like designers, designers should practice how to behave more like responsible marketers.

Marketing, then, is nothing more than selling art, right? Well, it's probably closer to selling "art with personal meaning" than it is selling "meaningless personal art." Regardless, the value of this art/meaning connection is real and here to stay, so if you need to hone up your art skills, do it now, but be sure to be clear about what you are actually learning. If you have perfected using all the filters in Adobe Photoshop but can't name the top five artists in the latest Venice Biennale, then you must realize the handicap this presents. Design is more than skill, and more than memorizing, it's knowing.

TREND
ENDER >>

10

THE INTERNET

IT'S CHANGING OUR LIVES

The Internet is perhaps the most influential and important development that most of us will ever see in our lifetime. The ability to talk about anything with anyone in the world is an amazing thing. But the very globalization that connects us can also bring with it a more disposable culture.

Think about this: New ideas can be shared instantly on the Internet or by e-mail. The fact that we can flash any image across so many eyes in so many different cultures homogenizes vision and taste to a point where masses can become desensitized. The Internet is the vehicle that is saturating the global mind so quickly that a new global culture can become anesthetized to once unfamiliar stimuli.

Past cultures were defined by national borders. There was a distinct connection between culture, art, religion and politics. Design today is relatively independent of such limitations, yet, in a strange way, it is even more connected via the Internet and media. These two vehicles allow for a deeper connection between niche groups, which cultural anthropologists call "experience clusters," because they are composed of individuals who experience like things together. At the same time, others may never even see what these niche groups are sharing. Early adopters can speed up the process of visual evolution within their group.

These redrawn boundaries of the human experience group us not by geography or national heritage, but by personal interests and desires. This is a rewiring of our social structure, a more individualized pattern amongst interest groups.

The scary thing is that something can only be new once. How long can this go on?

>>> *CHAPTER* 2

IS THIS THE END OF DESIGN?

In June 2007, I attended Documenta 12, a gigantic art show held every few years in Kassel, Germany. If the creative world had an Olympics, it would be Documenta. It has the power to affect global trends, and is often the first place where one sees the bizarre and out-of-the-ordinary visual leaders emerge. Often called the 100-day museum, it lasts through the summer and attracts nearly a million creative leaders from around the globe. It began in 1955 in an effort to reconcile German public life with global modernity. Today, Documenta features several pavilions throughout Kassel, each focusing on a noteworthy artist selected from one of the host nations. It's a great place for any creative to see where the future of art and design might be headed.

I always become excited about visiting such exhibitions, but this time the newspaper reviews were less than positive. Few artists shocked, experimented or caused controversy. More curious was the preliminary statement posted on Documenta's web site by the new artistic director, Roger Buergel, that sounded like a disclaimer. Was he preparing the visitors for the worst? "We conceive

of the exhibition as a medium that takes us away from the mere representation of the 'world's best artists' to the production of an experiential space." Heck, even the edgy art world is falling on experiential. What's left?

Even more disconcerting, the directors of Documenta 12 avoided establishing a clear theme; instead they arrived on three questions that set the tone. These questions, which they called leitmotifs, provide insight into the future of design, which, by the sound of things, is pretty scary.

1. "Is modernity our antiquity?"

2. "What is bare life?"

3. "What is to be done?"

Now, imagine yourself as an artist selected by your nation to create moving work for the entire art world to critique, based on those three questions. These three themes are not only intentionally vague, they are solid proof that even the most observant and powerful art evaluators in the art world are more than a little confused with what the future may hold for creativity. These leitmotifs are extremely similar to ones put forth by Adam D. Weinberg in his foreword to the 2006

p.50 >> The Vault49 campaign for Infinity cars was one of the first cases in advertising where decorative ornamentation was combined with vector silhouette graphics. p.51 >> *Left:* Vintage Ray Patin animation still from UPA, courtesy of Amid Amidi's Cartoon Modern web site. *Center:* This platter by New York designer John Derian uses vintage art. *Right, clockwise from top:* Platter with skates and manta

exhibition catalog for the Whitney Biennial, a highly influential exhibition for all creative people. He said, "Today's artistic situation is highly complex, contradictory, and confusing. It is an environment few can make sense of. The current state of affairs seems more complicated than ever given the sheer number of working artists and the morass of seemingly conflicting styles, conceptions, and directions."

As Documenta 12 and the equally influential global exhibitions like the Venice Biennale and the Whitney Biennial demonstrate, if the plan-

et's most influential curators and visual artists can't decide where things are going, how the hell are we supposed to? Perhaps this is the final nail in the coffin of design and art.

CULTURAL GROWTH

Cultural growth has been well documented throughout history, yet in this busy world most of us are still unaware of the impact early cultures have had on the development of others. For thousands of years, human cultures have grown, flourished and died, but not without first affecting other cultures. In our modern

rays, designed by John Derian. Vintage Ray Patin animation still from UPA, courtesy of Amid Amidi's Cartoon Modern web site. *Savoring Toby*, a painting by Gary Baseman.

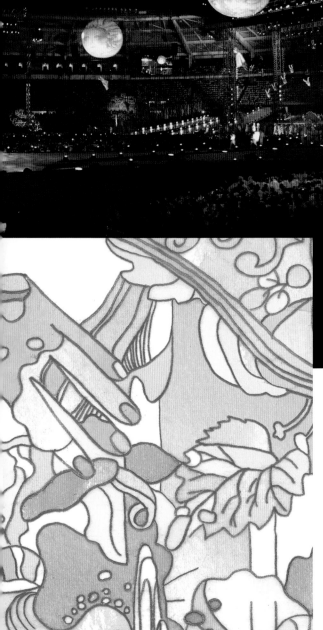

world, this is even more apparent with the connectivity of television and the Internet.

We must consider the impurity of our culture today, for it has evolved into a hybrid of everything that has come before it. Today, we continue to evolve with influences by cultures that came before us. Imagine the simple connection between our alphabet today and the one used by the Romans; architecture today and that of Ancient Greece; our food and Chinese cuisine; and the traditions of music that trace back to Italy. The influences are numerous and complex, and we work with them

p.52 >> *Top:* The opening ceremonies for the 2006 Winter Olympics in Turin, Italy, challenged each country to impress the world with its unique creativity and culture. *Bottom left:* Editorial illustration by Deanne Cheuk to accompany a Joanna Newsome album for *Fader* magazine. *Center right:* Still from an animated spot for Nike's "Embrace the Exotic" campaign, designed and created by design

every day. More importantly, as designers, we must realize that influences are continuing to affect design creation.

Historically, most cultural developments have evolved with distinctive arcs of creativity that are especially noticeable when viewed from the passage of time. Some of these you may be familiar with, such as the American arts and crafts movement, which was a direct response to the over-designed Victorian era. Go farther back in time, and we can see the same pattern with many visual cultures: the Incas, the Greeks, the Romans, the English of the Victorian and Renaissance ages, to name a few. Whether tiny trends or broad sweeping movements, the cultures all develop with strong idealistic roots, then move to almost opposing values.

Most visual movements seesaw through these periods of idealistic flamboyance successfully since the opposing movement always feels fresh and new. But things started to change in the late nineteenth century as communication improved and there were great developments in science and knowledge. People became less impressed by simple contradiction and they

and animation studio Lobo (www.lobo.cx). **p.53 >>** *Top left:* Another still from Nike's "Embrace the Exotic" campaign by Lobo. *Top right:* An animation still from an award-winning animated commercial produced for Brazil's Banco Real by the design collaborative Lobo. *Bottom:* Zaha Hadid's model for the aqua center for the 2012 London Olympics.

a reflective
solar top
- following
the -o
shading...

The
maypole
effect?

the
city
grid

The "city grid" is
really a 4-storey
increment, visually

The "city within a city" has
always been full of surprises!

began to demand more. Consider the amazing developments that arrived in the late nineteenth and early twentieth centuries. Enormous changes in perception occurred with advancements in science, mathematics, and lifestyle-changing inventions like electricity. These were the times of Thomas Edison, Charles Darwin and Albert Einstein, a time of invention and progress like no other.

Creatively, it was also a time of transition, a short period of time when things suddenly appeared old-fashioned in the face of newer technology. Between 1865 and 1938, the world

p.54 >> Lord Norman Foster's concept sketch for 30 St Mary Axe, his now famous London landmark building affectionately referred to as "The Gherkin." **p.55 >>** Can architecture be a brand? Lord Norman Foster comes as close as you can get to the idea of a "starchitect."

saw electricity, steel, and the automobile make sweeping changes in their lives. Plastics, air travel and packaged food followed. Consider the impact that the 1938 World's Fair had on design and culture, when the world first saw refrigeration, a washing machine and the highway. With television and radio connecting the planet, artists and designers began to speed their exchange of influences, from streamlining to surrealism.

Design as a concept moved in people's psyches from the more agrarian-minded consumer in 1900 to today's Internet junkie. The twentieth

p.56 >> *Top left:* Indoor Waterfall at Mohegan Sun Casino, Connecticut: America's largest casino. *Center left:* London rock concert or Mohican pride? Cultures are becoming blended so quickly that few know the difference between what's real and what's fiction. *Bottom left:* James Fenimore Cooper's book, *The Last of the Mohicans*—as well as the feature movie—led many to accept fiction as history.

century, which began with a single distinct visual movement, ended in a messy blur of multiplicity. In the end, it most resembled a continuation of modernism, and many concede that we are still in the midst of the movement. From the perspective of the far future, the entire twentieth century might be collectively defined as the period of modernism, broadly speaking.

Okay, we may be experiencing the beginning of an exciting new definition, but our current status also runs the risk of constant recycling for an undetermined period as culture waits for an effective disruption. Modernism or not, whatever we call the future, it is coming at us full speed, but we can't see it.

Branding Design

The design world has always appreciated greatness, while at the same time it teaches the audience to demand more and more every time. A supreme experience results in an expectation of a better experience the next time. We are ever moving the bar of excellence higher and higher. Culturally, we are obsessed with superlatives—the number one opera tenor, the

Right: London-based urban artist Ben the Illustrator has a unique style, drawing inspiration from peers such as Japan's Takashi Murakami and late twentieth-century graffiti artists. He combines this with the energy of edgier contemporary music, and we begin to see the emergence of a new urban hybrid style which may define the visual expression of today. **p.57 >>** Illustration by Ben the Illustrator.

best restaurant designer, the top chef, the hottest fashion designer, and the most important architect. We know these names: they appear on TV and in magazines, sell their products and do anything they can to market their names through various media.

Even the great cultural celebrations of our modern times now blur together in the mind. Take the opening ceremony of any Olympics. Once strongly cultural, the ceremonies now all seem similar, with only slight nods to the host nation's culture. As viewers, we expect reindeer in Norway's ceremony, native North American tribes dancing for Canada, the triumphant brass section of composer John Williams' fanfare for America, extraordinary elaborate Chinese fireworks and the finest Italian opera soloists. Our unique cultural expressions are most impressive when globalized, connected without boundaries. Some may label it the Hollywood or Las Vegas or Disneyfication of culture; others call it the celebration of expertise. But either way—is this over-information killing culture? Are there limits, or will we continue to break them?

p.58 >> Elevating today's over-vectored world of illustration to a more thoughtful expression of silhouette through authentic studio mediums like water color and fiber, New York designer Deanne Cheuk pushes beyond the norm with her innovative style. This is an invitation for an American Rag Cie store opening in Japan. **p.59 >>** Cheuk started stretching boundaries in 2005 as art director for *Tokion* magazine.

There is a reason why chef Emeril Lagasse has a restaurant at every hot location in Las Vegas and the Disney parks. We celebrate excellence and expertise. It's why we all know brands like Hard Rock Cafe, or resorts like Canyon Ranch SpaClub, and why they are not just at Disney World and Las Vegas, but at Target and on the *Queen Mary 2*. Today, design stars are everywhere; they collaborate with each other to create greater expressions, and their brands often validate a destination as "cool." If Downtown Disney has one, then Universal Studios City Walk must also. If London has one, then too must New York City.

Even simple ideas that try to remain small eventually become branded and risk reaching exhaustion through overexposure. Take the Got Milk? campaign or, better yet, the popularity of the Chicago Cows on Parade—those painted cows as public "art" that appear on street corners around the world. The original exhibit began in Chicago in 1999, and has triggered a global phenomenon that has resulted in painted dolphins in Miami and painted pigs in Cincinnati. The Cows on Parade brand itself is licensed to thirty-five cities worldwide, proving that if an idea appears simple and homegrown,

p.60 >> *Left:* The art of the hand today can be expressed through pen or mouse, as in Dan Funderburgh's invitation for Ninjas D'Amore, a pen and ink show at Gallery Nucleus, Alhambra, CA. *Right:* Dan Funderburgh's spread for *Overexposed*, March 2006. **p.61 >>** *Left:* "Tile Wars" poster by Dan Funderburgh. *Right:* A skull 'n' bones plate by New York artist John Derian.

DETAIL OF
"TILE WARS"
POSTER SOON
AVAILABLE AT
UPPER
PLAYGROUND
.COM

$$$

TRADE MARK

it is just as likely to grow to demand mass appreciation.

Global Pluralism and Natural History

As designers attempting to create "new," we face so many factors today that the task of invention appears more daunting than ever. As pressure mounts for us to create more and more things that appear new, there is one more factor to consider—the whole idea of globalism, or whatever we call the greater voice of a world that is now sharing most everything, instantly (see "Global Sameness" on page 22). Consider

for a moment what it used to be like before television and the Internet. Art movements rarely left the borders of a single nation.

I frequently like to draw analogies between design and natural history. There is something to be said about cultural expression, say, the way a particular ancient culture had a unique expression. There is a reason why museums of natural history document design and craft in their exhibitions. Why is it that today we forget the human element in design, the biology of it, what affects it in our world, and what allows for it to develop or become extinct?

If, as modern creators, we consider the future potential of human creativity, from primitive man to the cultural flourishes through the past 600 years and the recent speed at which design cycles have developed over the past 150 years, can we say with certainty that the future will continue to allow us to create more? No one knows the answer. But futurists can be proven wrong. All it will take is the introduction of something disruptive. It might be a newsworthy tragedy or the introduction of a new, yet unknown technology. Whatever it is, it must change the way we think.

Our present global pluralism can change at any moment for almost any reason, but currently there are few signs of significant change, beyond some exciting developments with architecture. Whether this is a good or bad thing remains to be seen, but as a designer myself, dipping for influence from the greater well of ideas, it sure appears that the well has gone terribly muddy. And digging deeper isn't the answer.

As human cultures merge in our modern world, cultural homogenization is becoming a very real possibility. One has to wonder

p.62 >> This poster design, by Jager Di Paola Kemp Design (JDK) of Vermont, was created for Flatstock, a poster show series presented by the American Poster Institute. **p.63 >>** Nagano City illustration for *Computer Arts* magazine by Ben the Illustrator.

what will be lost, and what we will decide to keep to pass on new generations; what we can really control, and if we will accept what we cannot. Culture growth is affected by design, and design is affected by culture growth, so designers are going to create one way or another. But I can't help but be curious about what will happen now that cultures are being consumed so quickly. Do we risk losing things worth keeping? As creatives, do we have a responsibility to know more about what we use from cultures as influence, as well as what we should introduce into modern cultures? Does design pose a risk to progress?

Or does it lead it?

Historically, there have been cultures that have been pushed aside, languages lost, artifacts dismissed. Certainly there have been cultures that never even left any record of their existence, so the basic idea that culture can be lost is not unknown. And these are cultures that might have lasted hundreds or even thousands of years. Now, think about today … our propensity for disposable everything. There is no time in history when people dismissed and adopted new modes of thinking so quickly.

As we redefine cultural development for the future, care and responsibility must be taken. Take the Mohican tribe, for example. Lost to time, virtually no one knows what that tribal culture was about. Yet, through the imaginings of the great and timeless book *The Last of the Mohicans*, James Fenimore Cooper—a novelist—has become our historian. Never intended as historical reference, today Cooper's fantasy has become our version of fact, our belief of the past. And then, add to that the mass media perpetuation of the myth with the indelible impact of film. The twentieth-century interpretation of Cooper's novel is probably all that

school children across the globe "know" of the Mohicans—either that or a trip to the Mohegan Sun Casino and Resort in Connecticut. It is our own irresponsibility to human cultural truth that has allowed this to happen, and to that I say, shame on us. And if you don't think the Mohicans are worth worrying about, flip forward a few dozen centuries and ask yourself, "What will the future believe as fact about us?"

Truth and Perception

Culturally, we expect truth in everything we do. Honesty, as a practice and a value, appears

p.64 >> Design for VH1 Soul by Vault49. p.65 >> Stereoscope house by Melbourne, Australia, architects Elenberg Fraser. Such star architects are in demand for iconic office towers and university libraries—as much as they are for residences and vacation homes, where people feel more confident expressing individuality and status.

p.66, p.67 >> This artwork was created by Brazilian artist Adhemas Batista to illustrate an interview in e-zine *NewWebPick*. Brazil is quickly becoming a world leader in contemporary design with its own graphic style. This style has been mined by the likes of Coke and Nike head creatives as they craft new expressions for their brands. This "Brazilian Effect"—intense color, sex and playfulness—

in most cultures and religions. Societies hold such truths as sacred, yet art has a tendency to poke holes in truths, and, ironically, art itself can play with truths and with perceptions, often successfully, especially in modern times, when anything is open and vulnerable to questioning. Human values and freedom are closely linked to our expression and development. That's why any attempt at censorship results in resistance.

Art and design is so powerful but it is all about perception. Consider controversial designs such as the Confederate flag, or the Nazi swastika. To some these are simple designed textiles; to others they represent pride; and for others represent oppression and hate. Even censorship means that there are strong feelings on both sides, otherwise no one would bother. This just proves the power human culture places on visual icons and design.

From the horrors associated with the black, red and white Nazi flag, to the ceiling of the Sistine Chapel, to last month's issue of *Vogue*, design is our ultimate human legacy. What will you leave behind as the truth of our times?

is injecting a new sensibility into global print ads, animation and video projects. **p.67 >>** Gary Baseman's instantly recognizable style may surprise some of his more conservative fans as he treats gallery goers with a unique take on fine art. *Hide and Seek Toby*, acrylic on canvas, by Gary Baseman, 2007.

UNCERTAIN FUTURE

Here is a hint that design might be over. The most respected evaluators of design, the foremost museum curators from the top world museums, can't find anything new that they can deem a "movement." The closest they can come is to label a collection as "contradiction."

So, are visual trends a thing of the past? Time may be the only thing that can save us. There are periods of stagnation that can last for decades, if not hundreds of years. It took as long as 250 years for human culture to evolve from the influences of the Renaissance to the

breakthrough designs of the Victorian era; twenty-five years between the modern and postmodern eras; and today, about five hours between "brown is the new black" and "black is the new brown." Designers today need to know the complete history of the creative world because they have little else to call upon. Not only are designers pressured to deliver new looks and styles that must excite and redefine the future, they are called upon to create them at an alarming rate. Seasonal design has replaced the phenomenon of trends. A short hemline may be in one season and gone the next, only to return the following

p.68 >> Constantly redefining modernity, London design firm ATTIK attracts clients who demand visionary ideas, and who reject clichés. When approached by Toyota to create a web site that connected with their Scion consumer, ATTIK came back with a game. The web site entertained visitors with trap doors and a cube-like world—and embraced the cool square-ness of the niche Toyota brand to the

season. The same can go for a color, a window treatment, a roof line, or a dance beat.

All creative professionals share a future that is unknown. The immense scope of accumulated knowledge being shared today, paired with instant global connectivity is both exciting and frightening and will lead to who knows where. And the "who" is the imperative here, because the "who" is "us."

For "us," I have one important piece of advice: Never expect to know the future. But demand of yourself the responsibility to create it.

And demanding it will be. The obstacles in your path are not only big; they are unprecedented. Here are just a few of the obstacles you will face in the foreseeable future of design ...

apparent delight of gamers, dudes, and Scion fan-boys everywhere. **p.69 >>** Dutch designer Marcel Wanders experiments and creates high concept and functional pieces. His objects are recognized worldwide by designers, museums and collectors. Here, his 2005 project with Italian tile manufaturer Bisazza Mosaico shows how contemporary designers and manufacturers can collaborate.

1

DESIGN IS NOW FOR EVERYONE

We've all heard it: The Democratization of Design. Good design is for everyone. But "good" won't be good enough for much longer. We've moved so far away from "form follows function" that we focused on form itself and tossed the function. To make matters worse, mass culture has forced form into becoming a mere commodity, and an ephemeral one at that. "I want it," "I got it," "I'm over it," "What's next?"

INNOVATION OBSTACLE »
2

CYCLES ARE FASTER AND SHORTER

Blame retailers.

Blame manufacturers.

Blame consumers.

Blame anybody you want, but the fact of the matter is, just-in-time inventory has rewired consumers to expect just-in-time style, too, and design is not a bottomless barrel—the bottom is in sight, coming faster than we think.

INNOVATION
OBSTACLE >>

3

TRENDS ARE A
GOOGLE SEARCH AWAY

You are not alone. The masses know what you know. Influence is everywhere, and can be anything that you want it to be. To stand out, you're going to have to create it, not copy it. And design will become more about the chef than the recipe.

INNOVATION OBSTACLE »

4

EVERYONE WANTS TO BE DIFFERENT

What else can we pierce on our bodies? Yet, it's not about the shock, is it? Anyone can do it. Big deal. See? With democratization comes homogenization. We are all different and all the same; we just don't feel different. Our schizophrenic modern life mixes everything up now. Nothing appears original or proprietary anymore.

INNOVATION OBSTACLE >>

EVERYONE CAN BE FAMOUS

The hell with different, be famous! Experience me! And now you can be famous, too. See you on MySpace. Think about it. You can design, lay out and publish your own book on Amazon.com now, and market it yourself right on the site. You can make a movie, post it on the web, land a sitcom deal and become famous simply through luck and proving your talent. Competition for design is not going away, it's getting greater.

INNOVATION OBSTACLE »

6

IT'S A D.I.Y. WORLD

Designers' tools are now available to everyone. If you thought your tattoo was proprietary, what about that new logo you are designing on your Mac? Do you know what is stopping your client from running down to the store to buy a logo design software program that will give him the swoosh he always wanted? I'll tell you what's stopping him—his daughter. She just skimmed *Photoshop for Dummies* and is ready to create the swoosh herself.

CLEAR ART MOVE- MENTS ARE GONE

Although Modernism arguably peaked in the mid-twentieth century, (some might say we are still in the movement), you can't argue that the most extreme expression of modern would be the minimalism of the 1970s—a blank white canvas, a Star Wars Stormtrooper. What feels new today? A singular, clear global movement remains indefinable. While others claim that deconstruction is a new movement, a greater question remains: What's next? The future of design is what we should be focusing on, not mining our creative past.

INNOVATION
OBSTACLE »

8

DESIGN IS NOW
A COMMODITY

Eek. There was a time when art would appear degraded if it even came close to business. The fact is that design has a vital role in business and economy, thus elevating the once superficial contribution of design as a purely artistic component to one that transforms and can disrupt a marketplace. The one thing everyone forgot is sustainability—not necessarily the sustainability of environmental resources (although those come into play, too), but the more ephemeral resources of originality and invention.

>>> *CHAPTER* **3**

LET'S INNOVATE!

While business is more or less putting a stranglehold on the advancement of design, there's an equal yet opposite compulsion amongst business leaders, strategic thinkers and business journals to strive for innovation. In the middle of the sea of sameness, business is just beginning to wake up. Executives all over the world are saying, "Holy cow! I need to differentiate." We can already see that creatively driven marketers can barely keep up with the desire for delivering the continual "newness" that today's consumer demands. It's no wonder that the corporate buzzword today is "innovation." In fact, it's already ubiquitous, appearing on the covers of annual reports, corporate web sites and in the hallways of the world's largest corporations. Savvy business leaders demand innovation from their management teams and hardly a business book or magazine doesn't have innovation on its cover.

So, make no mistake about it: business is suddenly beginning to "get it." And the future belongs to the talented.

Designers who exhibit extraordinary talent and who can create designs that influence are in the highest demand. The companies

p.79 >> Australian design collective Rinzen has worldwide clients like Puma, who seek out the group's distinctive, ever-changing mix of styles, techniques and art. The collective's members are based in Berlin, Brisbane, Melbourne and New York, and they work with clients from places like Japan and Copenhagen, redefining the idea of a local design firm.

that recruited MBAs from Harvard, Duke and Stanford yet hired creative staff via an ad in the Sunday paper have now revised their recruiting methods. Meet the future of design. Gone are the days of the art department. Welcome the new strategists of the future. The Fortune 100 companies who have figured out the value of creatives and who are providing exactly what they need are winning—and winning big.

Changing a company's culture is possible, but it's not easy and it certainly doesn't happen overnight. Attracting talent starts with significant change to an organization. If an underperforming creative team exists already, it is much more difficult to change the culture than it is for new companies that are just starting. For those with an entrenched culture, managers have to understand that it isn't good enough to click through a bevy of Photoshop filters that mimic rusted metal and call it a day. True "innovation" calls for the visionary futurist who is able to observe culture, combine examined influences and originate designs that are beyond trend and, even more, are culturally important. As companies shift their focus to a creative-centric future,

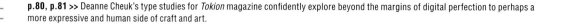

p.80, p.81 >> Deanne Cheuk's type studies for *Tokion* magazine confidently explore beyond the margins of digital perfection to perhaps a more expressive and human side of craft and art.

many will undoubtedly have an oil-and-water situation on their hands until the new set of expectations is installed and adopted by staff and management alike.

ATTRACTING THE RIGHT TALENT

In our digital world, we may have forgotten that historically there have been two distinctly different creative skill sets: technical and invention—both highly creative and talent driven, but using different sides of the brain. There are those who have an amazing skill to invent new ideas and expressions, and those who have an incredible technical aptitude and can make it happen. Many creatives will argue that they have both skill sets. Surely, most creatives today must be able to function in each, but it is the specialist who excels to a supreme level that has the potential to invent excellence.

The structure for the creative department of the future is an environment where all three styles can collaborate and thrive together.

Emotionally, creative people need the right environment to grow. And the challenge for design management is to provide it. Designers

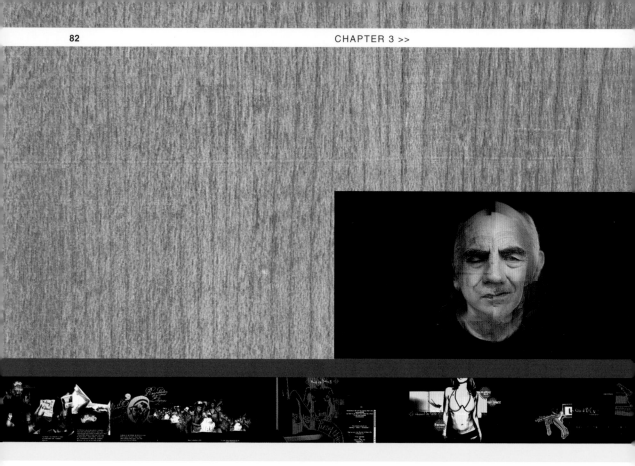

are a bit like precious greenhouse plants. You don't necessarily want the rare ones unless you need them, and you also don't want to mix cacti with moisture-loving orchids. Everyone has her place, and a restructuring of the idea of a creative group is no doubt going to be in order, perhaps even to the pre-Apple days of 1984, when the creative team was separated into two groups, mechanical and design.

In fact, there was good reason for the two different halves of the creative team—they used two different sides of the brain. Before 1988 and the extensive use of Adobe Illustrator, in design schools you could major in graphic design, and yet still migrate to one of two careers—creative designer or mechanical designer. Both are important roles to fulfill the creative delivery, but one is clearly a lead position, and one a technical support position. Today, creative designers are expected to have both sets of skills—both halves of the brain—but in truth, not all designers are equally talented in the two types of tasks. I would argue that taking the time of visionary, creative designers to require them to muddle through the technical specifications required

by their Illustrator or InDesign programs is a tragic waste of resources and another factor in the depression of design around the globe.

If one wishes to compete in the highly profitable world of style and fashion by defining the newest visual culture before anyone else has, the first step will be to create an environment where talent can flourish. Talent will avoid any corporate culture that tolerates underperforming creatives and mediocrity as an accepted standard in design. Many organizations don't realize their own weaknesses, especially when it comes to creative groups.

It may not be surprising, then, to see that some of the most innovative corporations that employ large numbers of highly talented people create environments that appeal to the opinion maker. Google, Nike, Hasbro, and Urban Outfitters have all designed workplaces that don't think twice about a tattooed neck or a skateboard outside the office. These companies know that the environment necessary for creative thinking must be free and open. Creative minds thrive in a culture where they believe, emotionally, that design is respected. This might be communicated through thoughtful details like flexible hours,

Coke, Milk and Cookies is quickly becoming a giant in the world of progressive visual design. *Top right:* A design for Culture Club web site, a site that not only promotes the hip Ghent, Belgium, music club, but is itself an entertaining experience. Site created by Milk and Cookies.

or Eames chairs in every office. Or it might be a lounge, top-notch espresso machines or after-hour cocktail parties. "Work" for creatives is not a 9-to-5 venture; it is a lifestyle. Creatives live and breath design 24/7, and thus, never turn off their minds. An accountant might check out at night, go home to his kids, and kick back and watch TV. A designer never turns off. The idea that they must plug in and turn on in the morning, as in a traditional office situation, is not as appealing. That said, combining creatives with other professionals in the same environment can be challenging.

Arguably, most creatives dream of being employed by the Apples, Martha Stewart Living Omnimedias and Nikes of the world, yet those organizations only hire the best of the best. What can we learn from them? Simple. Respect design. The corporation with the museum-worthy Noguchi coffee table and Frank Stella painting in the lobby is more likely to attract the artist with intellect than the one with framed photos of their own company's brands and products on display. Yes, that is important, but if you want to attract the most gifted creatives, their minds generally measure their success more on the

p.84 >> Logo designs for Diem skateboards by Budapest designer Karoly Kiralyfalvi. **p.85 >>** *Left:* A skateboarder practices in an Atlanta, Georgia, skate park. *Right:* Different cities all blur into a familiar scene, with automobiles, street lights, and commuters going home for dinner. This could be Miami or Berlin, but it's actually Hong Kong. *Background:* Rinse pattern, designed by Karoly Kiralyfalvi.

global playing field, rather than their own company's brands. They are proud of their contribution, but are more invested in design. They can identify the leaders in their field, and they measure success by their stature. Ego? You bet. All creatives want to feel good about where they work, but more importantly, they need to believe that their contribution is valued by not only their company but by global culture.

Just as the Walt Disney Company brands their Imagineers, and Apple labels their retail staff experts, the power of respect goes even deeper than a T-shirt and logo. What designer wouldn't want to be called an expert, or an Imagineer? The title demands instant respect. Feeling good about where a creative works is often the most important aspect of a job, since creatives rarely consider a job a job. Creativity is a 24/7 venture. Space and environment are equally important to the innovative creative process. The trend of studio-as-work space, which many of the most competitive creative businesses now promote, doesn't just make creative employees feel creative, it attracts attention and talent from the outside as well. And in this design-driven world that

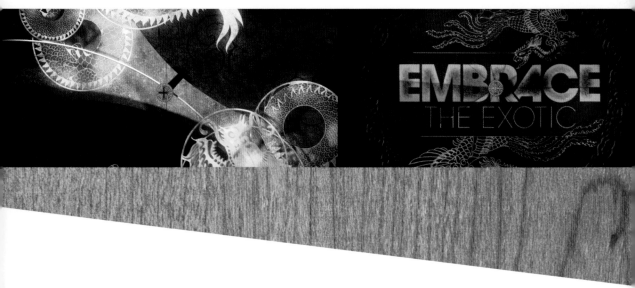

big business has become, that is often the bottom line—attracting talent.

The recent design of the amazingly creative-friendly campus for edgy-hip retailer Urban Outfitters demonstrates how collaboration and vision can have two results. Designers are getting an environment that is conducive to creativity, and the business is profiting from understanding the needs of their talent. Without the passion of Julie Bargmann, principal and founder of D.I.R.T., a business which finds beauty in derelict sites, Urban Outfitters could just as easily have found a

more average location for their world headquarters, and Philadelphia would not have repurposed the abandoned former Navy Yard. Today, the hundreds of talented creatives who design for the Urban Outfitters brands have an extraordinary work space that transforms the massive buildings, trains, and atmosphere of the Navy Yard into spaces where plaster squirrels and chrome cuckoo clocks are imagined, along with the piles of stylish hip clothing that define Urban Outfitters as a generation's leader in style and fashion. Along with award-winning architects Meyer, Borgman and Johnson, Inc.,

p.86 >> Stills from an animated spot for Nike's "Embrace the Exotic" campaign, designed and created by Lobo. **p.87** >> *Center:* Before Deanne Cheuk influenced the planet with her unique style, her early oil paintings provided hints of greatness. Oil painting from the Red

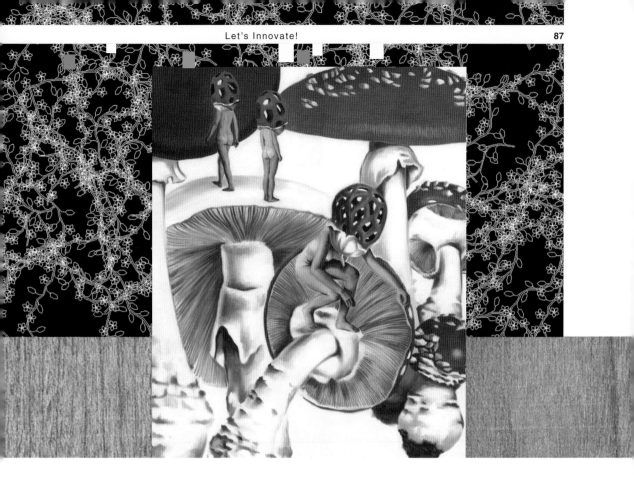

Ms. Bargmann helped create a space which is reaping awards, even winning the National Trust for Historic Preservation's National Preservation Honor Award in 2007. At Urban Outfitters, it is not only acceptable to stick things to walls, creatives are encouraged to create color palettes and display them for critique and to inspire a dialogue with fellow creatives. For the creative minds now graduating from a design school, Urban Outfitters' Corporate Campus is on the same list as Martha Stewart Living Omnimedia, Google's Googleplex, or Nike's Campus in Beaverton, Oregon. The creative minds thrives in good environments, and the message that they are respected is of utmost importance.

CREATING A CREATIVE CULTURE

If your business is struggling to understand its lack of innovation, you may not need to look at your creative staff but at your culture. The first rule in setting up an innovative culture is to allow for creativity, which often isn't a neat and tidy venture. You may argue that a professional environment must be maintained, and, certainly, most corporations enforce adherence to professional

Cap series, Deanne Cheuk, 2005. *Background:* Early digital work by the iconic Dutch designer, Tord Boontje, which in many ways feels just as new as the classic die-cut florals we all recognize today.

standards, but take a gander at the innovative company's creative departments, and the difference is fairly obvious. If you want to break rules and paradigms, you may have to tolerate a few more tattoos than you are comfortable with. They come with the territory. Remember, it's a different world out there—a connected world.

Word gets out amongst the other professionals. Designers share information on popular business networking web sites such as Linked-In and Vault.com, and creative networking sites like Coroflot, where creatives

post their resumes and portfolios, as well as share advice on the hot places to work and where to avoid.

Simply said, high-value creatives and their high-value ideas tend to leave organizations that don't "get it." We all can name the top companies to seem to get it, starting with Target. "Getting it" is really simple—it is having respect for design.

If designers are not happy, they will move on. There are always better places to go. But can companies afford to let their talent go, especially if they leave for the competition? Only

p.88, p.89 >> Stills from a Target commercial by Minneapolis design firm Catalyst Studios. **p.89 >>** *Bottom:* Tord Boontje's candelabra design for Target.

recently have the most competitive corporations realized that it is best to keep the creatives happy. Their redefinition of the "art department" has resulted in unconventional studios. But is it really that simple? Just let your creative teams do what they want and you'll get surprising results? Of course not. The reasons for the lack of design excellence in many creative groups are more complicated than that. Putting together an innovative staff involves an environment conducive to creativity, the right motivation and a creative culture. And that all begins with the people in control.

INNOVATION

Don't ask for the secret to innovation. That's the last thing you should do. So, for all the design mangers reading this, let's get this business out of the way right now. If you think that the answer to finding innovation is as simple as hanging a banner in the hallway and holding a pep rally that starts and ends with a call for innovation, you are mistaken. Let me repeat. You are mistaken. Creative people are not motivated by a demand, or by a new permission that, for whatever reason, it is now "okay" to innovate. Wasn't it accept-

p.90 >> *Top:* Escape skateboard design by Karoly Kiralyfalvi, Extraverage Productions. *Center:* Belgian design group Milk and Cookies' web site design for the indie flick *Ex Drummer,*

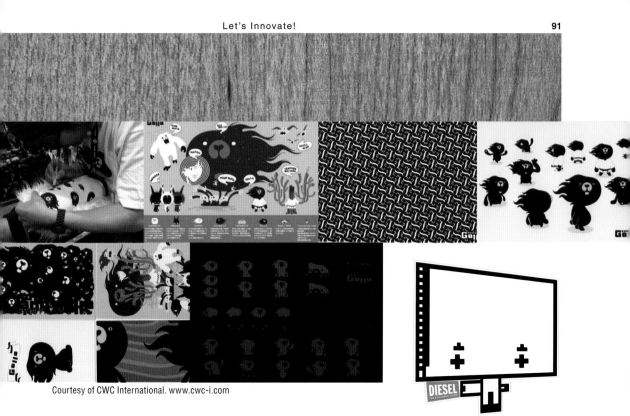

Courtesy of CWC International. www.cwc-i.com

able before? And if it wasn't, what on earth were you paying me for?

Clearly, one would be pressed to argue that innovation, as a business concept, could be perceived as a bad idea. The very definition of innovation is to find a solution to a problem in a way that is better. The word conjures up visions of new thinking, the promise of solutions that are new; thus, they must be better. It's a terrific challenge. Why, then, do so many creative people giggle and smirk when they hear the call of so many competitive companies? "Now is the time to innovate."

What is innovation anyway? I find the definition by IBM's John D. Wolpert to be most relevant to today's business and design challenged world. Wolpert leads IBM's Extreme Blue, an incubator for talent, technology and business innovation in Austin, Texas. He explains what he means by innovation as not "talking about processes for making improvements to existing products and services" and not "talking about purely technical invention." But instead, he defines innovation as "pursuing radical new business opportunities, exploiting new or potentially disruptive technologies, and

a film by Koen Mortier. *Bottom:* Seaweed plate by New York artist John Derian. **p.91 >>** *Top row and bottom left:* Character designs and illustrations by Japanese artist Akiyoshi Chino, courtesy of CWC International. All Rights Reserved. *Bottom right:* Design for a Diesel video project by design firm Milk and Cookies.

introducing change into the core concept of your business."

Certainly innovation falls within a process, even for creative talent who sometimes never think of the process at all since they are focused on the designing. When we focus on the more massive concept of disruptive change, things become a bit fuzzier. For one thing, creative people tend to be cynical about agendas that are pre-thought for them, and about most corporate speak, especially anything that comes remotely close to telling the creatives what should inspire them. There is

some psychology here worth exploring for a bit, and it may be something that has been developing over some time.

Since the late 1980s, and throughout the 1990s, corporate America experienced an enormous flux. Looking back, this period seemed relatively lucid and smooth from a growth perspective, but viewed from the early twenty-first century, we can see it was actually a transitional time of silent changes that no one noticed at the time, but which now appear to have led to our present drive for innovation.

p.92 >> *Crystal Magic* is an original piece by Jake Banks of Stardust Studios, Santa Monica, CA. **p.93 >>** This is an image from Microsoft Windows' "Start Something Big" campaign, designed by Stardust Studios.

Wouldn't it be nice if all that was needed for innovation were a gentle reminder that it's okay to innovate now? Permission granted. But there's a big problem. With all this talk about the need to innovate, no one talks about *how* to really innovate. The request for innovation gets passed down from on high to the creative group. If anyone is expected to innovate, clearly it is the most creative employees, right? Senior officers demand innovation from their highest executives, and they in turn demand innovation from their sales and marketing teams, and the marketers and brand managers demand innovation from their product designers, and the designers look to … well, you get the picture.

The hard reality is that when it comes to who must really initiate innovation, the task of asking for it starts not at the beginning, but at the end. The customer. The end-user. It's the consumer that really demands innovation, so why not just listen to him and just deliver what he wants? But that's not really a solution either. With today's improved communication systems and technology, information is shared in a nanosecond. Consumers edit and file information based on emotional responses,

and evaluate the worth of a site, brand or purchase in a moment. Click … "I like that" … click … "Hate that" … click … "Nice, but does it come in red?" … click … "Wow, love it!" … click … "Maybe eBay has a version."

This rapid connectivity has rewritten the book on how consumers adopt trends or dispose of them, thus driving marketers crazy as they seek the perfect lure. Staying competitive has evolved to reacting to trends. On the surface that sounds like the right thing to do, except in reality, reacting in the moment doesn't meet the development schedules for most companies. This resulting chaos illustrates what is happening today, as consumers demand something new, and business reacts. The challenge generally ends up on the desk of a creative—the innovator: "Create for me the perfect product that will make consumers believe that they needed it all along."

Since all this happens relatively spontaneously in the mind of the consumer, measuring the success of a new idea is difficult, if not impossible. This drives marketers and designers crazy. The quest to introduce market-changing ideas as world-shattering as the next iPod

p.94 >> Adhemas Batista, a self-taught artist who recently moved to Los Angeles from Brazil, has done work for some of the biggest brands in the world, including Coke, Nokia, Pepsi, Nordstrom and Microsoft. Havaianas banner design by Adhemas Batista.
p.95 >> Artwork created by Adhemas Batista for the Massive Territory Design Conference & Exhibition in Jakarta, Indonesia.

is at the same time marketers' greatest dream and their worst nightmare. Innovators must attempt the impossible: change the status quo and recreate a new one.

Which brings us back to the trend of innovation, for now we can see why business demands it. It has to in order to survive. The part that everyone leaves out of this impossible "process of demanding innovation" is where it begins and who must deliver it. Deep in the art department, in a tiny cubicle cluttered with urban vinyl toys and a frightening array of dark ephemera, sits a Mr. Potato

Head plopped on top of a monitor staring a brilliant mind straight in the eye. Meet the innovator. You.

Innovation = Function + Meaning

But that's what innovation means in the business model. What about what it means for designers?

The word innovation doesn't really mean much to designers anymore. Yet we must believe in innovation if we are ever expected to actually invent it. According to Scott Klinker, Designer-in-Residence at Cranbrook

Academy of Art, there are two definitions for innovation. First, "The solution must simply be better than the previous one, it should show improvement either functionally or visually." In other words, innovation is a functional, utilitarian advancement. But Klinker adds that innovation is also about "the significance of how the solution factors into the end-user's life."

In other words, as our fascination with starchitects demonstrates, form isn't enough after all. Real innovation is the marriage of improved function and significant meaning—

the 360 degree idea. In the design process, the focus is leaning more toward the positioning rather than the execution. The idea is king. The executional part can and probably will be outsourced, while the more proprietary part of the process—the creation part, the intellectual part—will remain inside, behind the protection of closed doors. Safe. Intellectual property management means much more than tangible, legal assets; it now also means ideas. These ideas can be manifested in many ways. But meaning is the true test for those who create against those who execute. Injecting real significance into an innovative

p.96, p.97 >> Advertising campaign for Puma by Rinzen of Australia.

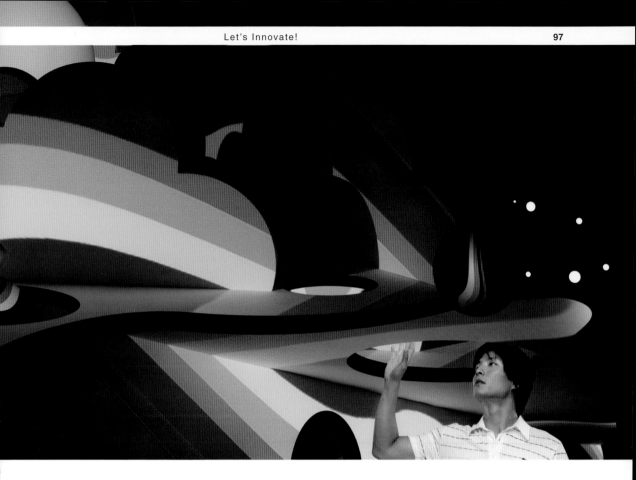

strategy is the key to meeting today's market demands. It is the factor dividing the old school model of design as a business solution and the new role of design as a contribution to art, culture and business.

Innovation as Culture Creation

Innovation has no relevance if no one needs it or if it doesn't have meaning to anyone. One aspect of creative invention that many forget about is its value. Not how much it's worth in a monetary sense, but how the idea contributes to the greater experience we define as culture. All creation is measured by time and purpose. If the idea never contributed to or moved culture, it was not really important.

New ideas advance culture in some way. Anyone who creates competitive creative work knows what I am talking about. The creative groups who figured this out are architectural firms, entertainment companies and film studios. These creative groups hire expertise, demand excellence and nothing less, and push the human experience forward since they master the full experiential effect. The

Walt Disney Company, for example, has mastered the full experience. Visit one of their theme parks to see how this effect has little to do with a ride on a roller coaster. It's also a restaurant, a nightclub, a hotel or a resort. It's why Las Vegas is popular with a new generation—we can't help but be seduced by the execution of great creativity.

Thinking of designers as culture creators helps us reexamine the mission and figure out what skills are necessary to undertake it. Understanding the fundamental traits of those talented creatives who have the potential to become culture creators, or even culture curators, is key to attaining authentic innovation.

p.98, p.99 >> Various Hasbro property concepts, designed by the author.

>>> CHAPTER 4

A NEW CONSUMER

High culture, low culture, pop culture, any culture—they all conjure up preconceived perceptions that one just can't address in a small book about visual trends. Hell, the word "trends" is equally laden with baggage and perceptions, as is much of the other descriptive design lexicon, such as "fashion," "cool" or "style."

Everyone has a set value system when evaluating anything visual. The value system is not always a conscious choice, though it affects how each of us reacts or is informed by the culture. One of the great things about

design is that it can move people to emotionally react to it. Since creatives are more culture creators than merely designers, they must be aware that they are affecting how people will react to their work. As customers change how they adopt design into their lives, so must creatives. They take on the added responsibilities of knowing why they created something, whom it is for and where their creative influences are coming from.

Things move so fast today that we even talk about design and what it means to us differently. Previous definitions of our visual world

p.101 >> Art from Los Angeles artist Dan Goodsell's Mr. Toast and Friends Exhibition, shown at Monkeyhouse Toys in Silverlake, California, March 2008.

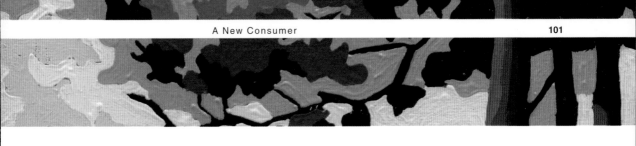

can seem outdated. Descriptors such as "elitist" or "trendy" may dismiss a concept instantly—or validate one. Not long ago, an elitist brand would feel outrageously out of place, but today, we talk about luxury brands as simply another category. We accept the idea of a range of consumers without the prejudice we once held. It's okay to buy a thousand dollar purse if you donate five hundred dollars to your children's book fund at school. It's okay to buy a Prada suit, because everyone should have one nice suit for job interviews. We justify our elitism, and we are more comfortable with trendy items, since we look at them as necessary disposables that help connect us to our tribe. "I need a Blackberry, since everyone at work has one and I don't want to appear like a neo-luddite." Other factors, such as perceived quality or value, can also be measured in opposing ways. We now hear of terms like "masstige" (mass prestige), or "mass customization." Some brands can even be defined as "aspirational luxury." There is no escape from the meaning that visual design brings.

Businesses and brands know who their consumers are. Many brands have a split demo-

p.102, p.103 >> Brazilian design firm Lobo was founded by Mateus de Paula Santos and Nando Cohen. These frames are stills from an early client, a local radio station in Brazil, which proves that even in 2002, the world was about to get the first dose of what was then

graphic base, especially if they are luxury brands. Both low- and high-income people can adopt the same brand. Consumers struggle to both "belong" and to "express their individuality." In the process, they develop new ideas such as "mash culture"—the idea that one can cherry pick from a wide selection of choices in an effort to create a new identity. Some experts argue that mash culture is a reaction to the democratization of design; I believe that it is a direct result of the phenomenon. Mash culture even elevates the entire design-is-for-everyone movement and delivers faux individual-

ity composed of brands regardless of their social position.

This combination of false luxury brands combined with other mainstream brands is quickly becoming the only way of expression in a world with an abundance of valueless choice. I call this high pop culture—a strange mash of elitist brands, faux brands, quality brands and almost anything else, though, most likely, a brand. This is most often expressed through fashion, but the same is happening in music, interior design and product design.

known as the "Brazilian Wave"—a unique characteristic blend of many elements and cultures. Who could have predicted that this also would be the perfect recipe for today's global mashing?

MASH CULTURE

High culture refers to elitism experienced by only the privileged few in Europe, beginning in the seventeenth century and extending into the early twentieth century. Cultured Europeans took the Grand Tour, traveled to Paris to commission haute couture clothing and supported the master painters in Florence. It was a balance of quality education and exposure to high art and literature that was intended to lead to a communal sense of pride and purpose. It was meant to uplift the entire culture. But once American progress began to rise around the turn of the twentieth century, things changed. The class system in Europe remained less challenged, but it was a different story in America. Today, design is more accepted in most European cities, as is modernity. In America, things are slowly changing, especially with the younger generation, but outside of the bigger cities, there continues to be a perception that good design is simply a European ideology (i.e. leave the fancy food to the French, give me a steak).

Large cities are different as they phase into three and four generations of culture mixing.

p.104 >> Painting by urban pop artist Tim Biskup. **p.105 >>** *Left:* Painting by Tim Biskup. *Right:* Still from Cartoon Network's animated program *Foster's Home for Imaginary Friends*, created by a wide range of twentieth century influences that together define the look of a new century in animation.

Boston, New York and Chicago are increasingly like London. These Euro-ethnic populated cities are comfortable with the idea that good design and art are important to the enjoyment of life. High culture is still held with regard, especially in the older European cities. In Paris, it is part of everyday life for anyone—from a repairman to an executive—to take a long, slow lunch, which may last two or three hours, consisting of artisan bread, rich red wine and some cheese. In their culture, that is as common as meatloaf and mashed potatoes might be to a working-class American. But who could have predicted that mashed potatoes could lead to mashed culture? Perhaps it was inevitable.

As high culture thrived in Europe, America evolved quite differently, and very quickly. A hundred years ago, the great East Coast cities, New York and Boston, revolved around a fabric of rich heritage brought over by immigrants. Life was based around family and hard work, but it was uniquely American. Steel mills, coal mines and automobile manufacturers became epicenters for a new cultural stew. In cities like Chicago and Pittsburgh, American and European values

blended—French, Jewish, Lithuanians, Polish, Chinese, Germans, all separated by neighborhoods, but increasingly connected by shared values. America's culture formed around the promise of hard work—a necessity-based culture of function over form—with no time for high culture when there was a good day's work to be done. Even today, cultural conservatism reigns, from small New England villages to rural townships in the South to farms in the Midwest. Value is still seen as simply saving money. The perception that good design means unaffordable and wasteful elitism still exists, yet we know

that a new, informed generation is emerging even in the most culturally cautious corners of the United States.

Needless to say, the consumers who are changing the fastest are kids. No one can culture-mash as fast as they can. Today, kids follow the World Cup as well as the NFL. Tweens—those between the ages of 8 and 13—are as comfortable with a Coach store as they are at a hot dog stand at the mall; they eat goat cheese *and* American cheese; they wear Levis and eat sushi; and they carry authentic Louis Vuitton bags with their Forever

p.106 >> New York designer/artist Julia Rothman creates original patterns and designs for textiles, wallpaper and the toy industry that appeal to a new generation of consumers who connect with her unique sense of craft. With clients like Urban Outfitters and Hasbro, one can find Julia Rothman patterns throughout the home. **p.107 >>** Fabric print and dog bed by Julia Rothman.

21 outfits. Cultural convergence is not only unavoidable, it's happening in your hometown, at all levels.

Accessibility to high culture has met a mass-market mentality joined with technology-enabled, speed-of-light pop culture trends and has emerged as something brand new: high popular culture—today's culture, in all of its expressions, blended together as one.

ACCESSIBILITY TO GOOD DESIGN

What was once the sole province of a select few trend forecasters, designers and top studios is now available to everyone. Humans have achieved a new standard of knowing—a standard that knows no borders, culturally or figuratively. Now everyone can make value decisions based on sound bites of scattered information, thus creating a world of over-informed consumers who evaluate an over-abundance of visual information against their own personal criteria—a whim-based decision-making process, if you will. We can change preferences at our fingertips anytime we like. We make choices based not on entrenched values, such as what our parents taught us, but instead on what feels right at the moment. We have

p.108 >> Chandelier plate designed by Julia Rothman. p.109 >> Tablestories plate by Tord Boontje.

entered a new phase of consumer behavior—consumers without context.

It no longer matters where you live. A fashion design student in the Philippines can choose to view a Valentino couture fashion show live if she so wishes. How much will that influence her designs? But wait, a tribesman in East Africa could have access Valentino's show too, as could a turnip farmer in western Yunnan Province in China. We are all visually privileged now. Good design has gone mainstream.

And as it does, we are faced with new sets of questions for ourselves as designers.

What are we left with? If everyone has access to everything, what will influence us in the future? Where will we find "new"? Is there room for a continuation for visual growth in this kind of environment?

Loss of Meaning and Individuality

Another phenomenon driving visual change is the related loss of meaning and individuality as global cultures merge and blend. We are inherently curious and love to discover and explore, but, as humans, we are also concerned—if not obsessed—with perception and

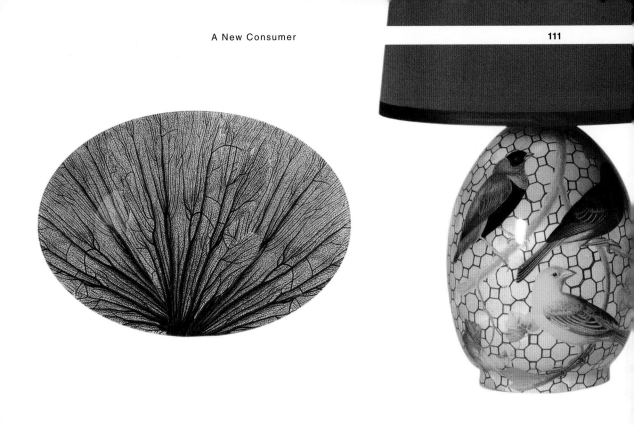

appearance. Individuality and belonging may seem to be contradictions, but they are powerful emotional drivers in how humans evaluate cultural information. Consider fashion and style, two of the design world's most volatile and powerful expressions. Where could they be going now that everyone can buy exactly the same pair of chinos at Gap and it doesn't matter if you're in Tokyo or Boston?

Design is driven more by fashion these days, where style is more of a factor than quality. But that has not always been the case. In fact, early innovators of the last century were driven by a core philosophy that avoided elitism—the belief that good design came purely from function. Aesthetic value was considered something for the wealthy and unnecessary for the everyman. Utilitarian designers focused on function. As commerce grew, mass market soon meant not only poor visual design but poor quality too, since business rarely invested in the aesthetic appearance of low-priced products. Rarely did design deliver both values because it didn't have to.

Today, I can walk into any Target store in America and buy a butter dish designed by

p.110 >> Platters by John Derian. John Derian creates plates and other home goods using influences from the worlds of science and art. His tendency to juxtapose images from eighteenth and nineteenth century illustrations with modern tableware defines his unique style.
p.111 >> *Left:* Platter by John Derian. *Right:* Lamp by John Derian.

p.112 >> *Top:* Pressed Flowers, an early design for curtains by Tord Boontje. *Center:* Little Flowers Falling by Studio Tord Boontje. *Bottom left:* Who says a speaker needs to look like

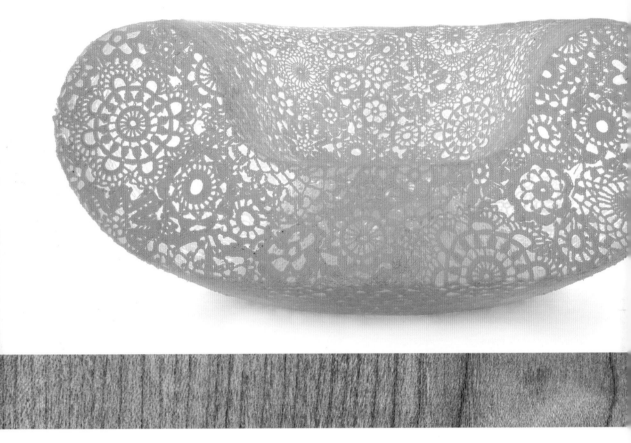

architect Michael Graves. It's functional, of course—it holds butter. Yet somehow that's become not enough. Now what matters is how it looks while it holds the butter … and what it says about me.

The availability of good design to anyone is called democratization of design. But here's the quandary. Because any of my neighbors can now buy exactly the same butter dish, does it actually say anything about me at all? It leaves me wondering: Does the ability to acquire a once unaffordable luxury such as high design make it lose its appeal, or is this

a necessary rite of passage in humility and ethics towards a better future of socialized design? I want to believe that we as a culture can achieve both. Why not? Everyone deserves good design. We have been trained to want symbols of status and now we can have them. But the elitism of having something not available to others is disappearing.

That may not seem like much of a concession, but it is only part of the cost of this democratization of design. If everyone has access to quality design, how does a designer stand out? This may be great for the consumer, as they

a speaker? Satellite speaker by Marcel Wanders. *Bottom right:* Petal chairs by Jon Racek and Kevin Racek of Stew Design Workshop, Burlington, Vermont. **p.113 >>** A chair that looks as if it is crocheted of lace is perfectly executed juxtaposition, and is often enough to make something feel new today. Crochet Chair by Marcel Wanders.

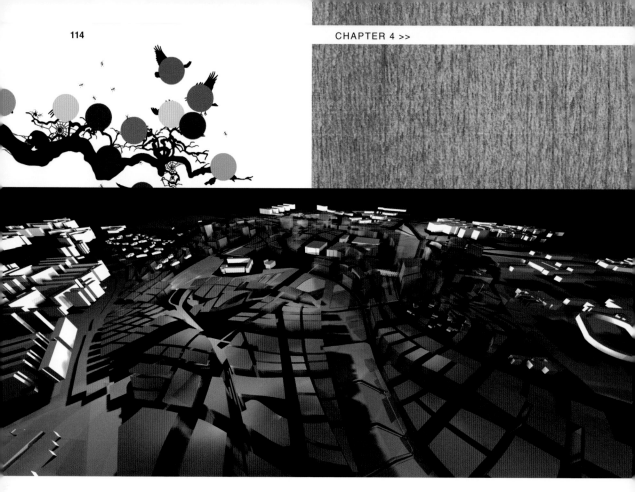

get better value and quality, but it means that designers have to strive harder to be noticed amongst the competition. What at first seemed like a new ideological position, delivering a new strategic position for competitive businesses, may be turning in on itself.

So the industry looks to us, the creatives, to tell them what comes next. This is your job. If you get nothing out of this book except this, let me spell it out: *You* must have an informed, intelligent and effective answer to the question of what is next. Anything less and you are not a designer.

Which leads to the phrase that is missing from the language of design spoken by business today, two words that will come back to bite you if you aren't in pursuit of them each and every day: design excellence.

So what can you do about it? Where can you look? Is it possible to continue to produce anything new? Is anyone seeing a promising future for design? The answer is yes. The future of design is not dead. It is merely transforming in front of our eyes into a brand new place, one where we can let go of our past baggage and be free to create without limits.

p.114 >> *Top:* Illustration by Rinzen. *Bottom:* Pritzker-Prize-winning architect Zaha Hadid's study for One North, an urban plan for the Science Hun Development Group (SHDG), Singapore. Achitecture may be the leading creative field where the future is beginning to emerge: the practice of using the computer not as a tool, but as a brain. Today, the connections beween biology and design are even more apparent,

and when the computer is used as a brain, it may help us overcome roadblocks such as cliché and assumption. As architects are discovering, who ever said we needed a flat wall and a pointed roof? The computer may show us that nature can teach us more than we could ever imagine on our own. **p.115 >>** "The Music Tree," an illustration for a Camel Cigarettes direct mail piece by Vault49.

>>> CHAPTER

THE EXCELLENCE
IMPERATIVE

We all have heard the phase "gifted artist"—and to an extent, it does feel like a gift. But talent requires careful training and management in order for it to properly develop. Call it a gift or a burden, the inner need to design—especially when paired with a highly developed intellect and talent—is rare, and not something that can be taught through *Photoshop for Dummies*. Tools and rules are important, but are only part of the recipe that makes a designer a designer.

I remember in the 1980s that my family worried that I would have no future because I decided to major in fine arts. Yet who could have predicted the sudden need for creativity that we are experiencing today? The world needs talented designers; it most likely always will. But don't be fooled, not everyone recognizes the gift we bring.

We practice creativity in a time when design and talent is in the greatest demand by business, so why is there also a flattening of design and a disregard for the industry? Design has never been more respected and in demand than it is today, while at the same time it has also never been more disrespected

p.117 >> The elements of Chicago artist Jill Dryer's illustrations may be informed from an intellect that clearly understands design heroes and movements gleaned from a century of creative influencers, but the painting still says, "I get it, don't you?" to the hip, informed opinion-maker who buys such work because of the obvious intellectual sensibility it demands.

and abused. (Or is it disregarded and made superficial?)

AUTHENTICITY AND EXCELLENCE

The creative experience is being redefined before our very eyes. Design and everything we learned that goes into the mysterious process that leads to innovation is the golden ticket and everyone is attempting to say that they have it. But who really does? And, if anyone does, how can one measure the excellence of something as intangible as design: Isn't that just judging an idea? If we are ever to prove to

p.118, p.119 >> My Little Pony meets Coke? Perhaps, but that's exactly why it appeals to a particular audience. Coke hired five design experts from around the world, led by the Designers Republic (tDR), to develop a brand vocabulary called "Love Being." tDR founder Ian Anderson states, "Big brands like Coke are finding that blanket advertising is no longer an option: It's both expensive and ineffective."

the rest of the world that our talents and skills are truly beyond trend thinking, then we need a redefinition. Trends are over. The future is all about something that is more meaningful, more tangible, more real. The future is about authenticity, and it's about design excellence, and I argue that authentic design excellence can be defined, measurably, if the creator can cite influences from authentic sources. Remember: Little is new, and much of what we assemble comes from something else.

It is our responsibility to recognize why something influenced us, and why we identified it

as an influence. This is not easy, by any means, since it requires a great amount of work, but it can be done. For example, one can say that graphic repeat forms, as seen in recent pierced fabric panels appearing at interior design and furniture shows, might be influenced by the work of Dutch designer Tord Boontje's laser-cut cascading floral sculptures, which, in turn, may have been influenced by the early vector silhouettes of contemporary artist Ryan McGinness's art installations. I might predict that combined with computer graphics, repeat vector shapes may be the next logical expression of the current decorative silhouette

p.120 >> *Left:* As brands look for greater meaning, companies like BMW hire superstar architects to create destinations for their brand. Rendering for BMW Welt, Munich, Germany, designed by architectural firm Coop Himmelb[l]au, Vienna, Austria. *Right:* Architecture firm Elenberg Fraser, led by directors Zahava Elenberg and Callum Fraser, pairs talented recent graduates with professional architects

to ensure that the freshest ideas blossom. **p.121 >>** Red Wing Worx logo designed by Dan Baggenstoss of CAPSULE, Minneapolis, MN. The PUSH Institute logo designed by Greg Brose of CAPSULE. America's Team logo designed by Brian Adducci of CAPSULE. Tenet logo designed by Greg Brose. Buck 'n' Jims logo designed by Brian Adducci. Handi Medical Supply logo designed by Greg Brose.

movement seen in many Target store commercials, and Coke's web site. I may even note that the dinner service design of Vera Wang elevates this movement by fragmenting the forms with knock-out white lines that are repeated across the images on her plates and cups.

The problem isn't whether people understand your work: The challenge you face is to research and sell your idea. I always challenge other designers by saying that if they cannot tell me how they arrived at a solution, the solution may not be valid. Informed design is not the same as plagiarism, but accepting uninformed design is more dangerous. I call this Random Design. It's not thoughtful and it's not conscious. Creatives who arrive at solutions by pulling random influence out of thin air, or by mimicking what they saw at the mall, will have designs revealed to be inauthentic, a hollow response, or a cliché that has been expressed before. Then the gates are open for the truly talented individual who has the special gift of connecting the right insights and influences into meaningful expressions.

The shift toward creative excellence has begun. Are you ready for it? The challenge now is

p.122 >> Lund Food–Byerly's logo designed by Brian Adducci and Greg Brose of CAPSULE, Minneapolis, Minnesota. **p.123** >> *Grey Type*, illustration by London artist Alice Stevenson.

how to move forward if this is new territory for you. As those faux creatives drop like flies, the vacuum left behind will demand fast and brilliant designers to create groundbreaking visuals. It's up to you to invent the innovation part of this challenge. We creatives need to rewire ourselves in order to relate to a business world desperate for true visual excellence, but which fears anything truly new.

First, if you are expecting to get a checklist on how to innovate, put this book down. You're not going to find that here. Sure, I can say things like, "Start a tickler file with your favor- ite clippings from magazines," or "Take a field trip to a museum." There are dozens of books out there with INNOVATION on the cover. Get them. Read them. Then tell me if you are inspired. True creativity is inspired by a zillion different things, and is extremely personal and often different for each and every creative. I can't even think of two creatives I have ever met who were inspired by the same exact thing. Business managers, relax. Innovation is easier than you think. If you have a group that is not inspired, sure, something is wrong. Consider this—no one ever needs to inspire an artist. There is a reason why artists continue

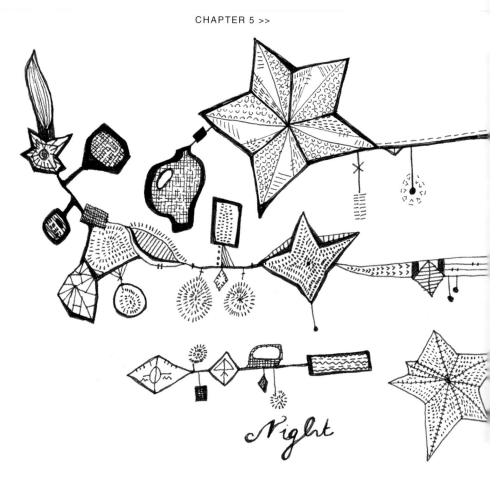

to create in prisons, or under a dictator's rule. How bad can your business be?

Creating Beyond Trend

As the world of business (and consumers) continues to raise the bar on design, you, the creative, are in the esteemed position of delivering what will eventually change the world. While business books are published all the time boasting that the authors know what consumers want or why some ideas are better than others, this book has really one mission—to inspire you to release the shackles of your

past and free-fall into the gorgeous future of uncertainty. We creatives love uncertainty. We thrive on it. It inspires us. What do you have to lose? Worst-case scenario is that we just end up where we are right now!

The future of invention is not over. If anything, we are at the cultural beginning of something great, we just can't see it yet. Even though many will look to history for examples of what may happen, I'm not convinced it is that simple. Although history has trained us to view development along paths—a linear logic—I believe that, given today's complex world, the process

p.124 >> *Lines*, an illustration by Alice Stevenson of London. **p.125** >> *Purple One*, an illustration by Alice Stevenson.

that leads to visual innovation is changing. As a naturalist, I am seeing more and more similarities in nature and our environment as examples of how scenarios might play out. Nature herself appears very linear on the surface, but as human intellect grows over time, we are continually surprised by what we don't know. Factors affect nature in strange and yet still undiscovered ways. Scientists cannot even agree on the factors leading to global warming. The future development of visual design is, in a very real way, as phenomenal as nature. Design is entering a phase of non-linearity, and so is becoming more fascinating, more rare, more respected and more desired. Okay, we can't really control it, but we can at least learn from it.

Design is valued more today than ever before. Already we are starting to hear about lead creatives as superstars, the same way we hear about sports figures or medical breakthroughs. For instance, top Pritzker-Prize-winning architects are sometimes referred to as "starchitects." A structure designed by Zaha Hadid or Frank Gehry is seen as a way to validate a leading university or growing city. It doesn't matter if the building leaks or isn't habitable; the design is valued as an object. One thing

p.126 >> *Structure of Reality*, illustration by Alice Stevenson. **p.127 >>** Urban architecture that exploits the shape of the natural landscape has been a consistent theme within the career of Zaha Hadid. This proposal for an urban master plan for a new quarter in Singapore applies the concept of artificial landscape formation, matching forms and structure to the topography rather than following the unnatural that proves that design has become more powerful is that function often follows form. And to be honest, I'm not afraid to admit that I'm fine with that in these cases.

The experience is often more powerful than the purpose. Anyone who has worn an uncomfortable pair of embarrassingly expensive shoes knows what I mean. They might give you blisters, but if they are absolutely stunning it's worth it. Experience often defies the old-school idea of function being paramount. It may seem superficial to admit this, but sometimes beauty does matter. Sometimes the visual experience is as important or more important than what it achieves.

Today, universities hire starchitects to build their libraries and concert halls simply to make a statement. It says, "We are so important that we are noteworthy." And people stop and pay attention. One can't help but notice the noteworthy, since being noteworthy today is extremely rare.

Aspire to Be Noteworthy

Designers have the ability to make something noteworthy. If you have the proven talent to

geometry of straight streets and structures. As modern architecture releases itself from traditional rules of logic and boldly moves toward a more integrated and informed design process, the entire future of design may benefit.

ZAHA HADID

create noteworthy contributions to design, than there is no better time to be creating. The best creatives strive for greatness; they can't help it. Ego and design are closely linked. The drive that pushes one to greatness is fed by the ego. These driven people are the noteworthy creators who stand out from the rest.

Some creatives dismiss the contributions of noteworthy creators, because they label them a Design Stars, or as brand-obsessed opportunists exploiting their profession by formulating design. Some of this might be true, but it is hard to argue with outstanding achievement in the arts given our climate of sameness. You don't have to like what they create, but you must recognize it for its ability to reach forward. Noteworthy design is not about simply being different; it's about creating a new space for dialogue. It creates new context for all creatives to feed upon. I am always amazed that so many creatives don't know their art history or the great creative minds of the past, but I am even more shocked at how many don't know their peers, the current recognized leaders of the design world. If you are on a mission to create the "new," then aspiring for greatness is hot-wired within you, and you can't even

p.128 >> The work of noted architects today is celebrated in much the same way that the other cultural icons are—it is awarded a major museum show. Installation view of Zaha Hadid, Solomon R. Guggenheim Museum, New York. p.129 >> A detail of the architect's model for Phare Tower, a Paris skyscraper designed by architecture firm Morphosis.

begin unless you know who has tried, what has been done already and whether they hit or missed. How else can you know where you are going creatively?

CULTURE CREATORS

Just as artists are driven to create, creatives are driven to design in a way that provokes a response, but they rarely focus on the process of design. The process is the craft. Artists are driven to create significant contributions, whereas craft-focused creators are more in-tune to the physical aspects of

design. Both can be significant, and creativity can contribute to culture in many ways, but not all contributions can be significant. Some are culture enhancers reinforcing a current expression—those who play with emotional connections with the past, vintage, reminiscences and meaning. Design can push both boldly forward into the unknown, or confidently and fearlessly back in time. Both can be exciting, and combinations of these influences actually define the current movement that began in the early 2000s. As design learns complex new patterns, it plays with time and space.

Perhaps the real opportunity here isn't innovation, but cultural movement. It's all about the ultimate contribution to the greater thread of cultural development. Talk about significance! Cultural contributions change the world.

Self-Evaluation

Ultimately, we all must look at ourselves and ask the hard questions. Where are you on the train of cultural development? The roles on this track are many: there are engines, passenger cars, fuel cars, and then there are

p.130, p.131 >> The Phare Tower in Paris is more than just another green skyscraper: When it is completed in 2012, it may very well be a landmark for the design world with its three-hundred-meter façade of undulation and smooth form. Designed by architecture firm Morphosis in Santa Monica, CA.

those who lay the tracks. All are creative, all are necessary, and all must function with excellence to ensure that the train continues forward. The safest place to sit is right now, and it is your job to remain there, informed, current, fresh, sharp and smart. You don't have to be an expert, you only have to create well-informed work—which, when you think about it, is a pretty hefty task in itself. Generally, this is not a problem for us creative types, since we thrive on absorbing culture and staying current.

Evaluating Expertise and Talent

As a creative leader in a major corporation myself, I am often asked to evaluate visual design, and sometimes the human element as well. Evaluating designers, art directors and any creative person who contributes to the design process, as well as the work that they produce, can be rather sensitive, as it involves egos, opinions and feelings. Anyone who has to evaluate talent knows the challenges this presents. If you are responsible for managing a creative team, I suggest doing the following:

p.132 >> A tattoo design for *Tattoo Icons*, a book that challenges traditional tattoo design. Created by Rinzen for Victionary 3, it was designed for the book's release at the first Pictoplasma animation conference in Berlin, Germany. **p.133 >>** Visual design for Havaianas campaign by Adhemas Batista.

1. Evaluate your culture.

2. Evaluate who is evaluating design.

3. Evaluate your talent.

Since design factors into the evaluation process, you can use the measurement of success in the marketplace as a guide. But that only gives you one measurement of worth, not the complete picture. To aid in the evaluation of creatives, get some other viewpoints. Bring in experts from the outside—not design groups or consultants but recognized visual leaders—to evaluate your visual solutions. Claudia Kotchka of

Procter & Gamble says that bringing in a panel of visual experts once or twice a year helps the creatives to overcome the "I like" syndrome. An internal review conducted by industry experts is an opportunity to educate your creative staff with unbiased feedback. Any time designers articulate their influence and direction, they grow new synapses, learn to design in the moment and becoming increasingly aware of where their ideas are coming from.

A board of visual experts can be assembled from a speakers list gathered from any leading design conference, such as the HOW, AIGA,

---

p.134 >> *Left:* Neon sculpture by contemporary artists TJ Norris and Scott Wayne Indiana. *Right:* Packaging design for Ponyloaf CD, *O Complex,* by Rinzen. **p.135 >>** *Left:* Packaging for Xiu Xiu CD, *Fabulous Muscle*s, by Rinzen. *Right:* Packaging for The Incredible Strand CD, *The Incredible Strand,* by Rinzen.

XiuXiu
FabulousMuscles

THE INCREDIBLE STRAND

or TED conferences, or from the list of judges printed annually in any of the leading design magazines, including *PRINT*, *HOW*, and *I.D.*, *The International Design Magazine*. Proceed carefully, though. Remember that there are many who will claim to be visual experts. Who wouldn't? I can't think of a design firm or an individual in the design business that would admit otherwise.

Then, of course, there is the portfolio. It is important to review the portfolios of not only the entry-level designer, but the creative leaders as well.

The Digital Boomer Effect

Digital boomers are early adopters of digital design technology, those who converted in the mid-to-late 1980s and early 1990s. I admit that I am a digital boomer, but I am also an artist. I have always believed that the computer is a tool, not a brain. (Notice how I called it "the computer"? Key phraseology of a digital boomer!)

As an artist at J.S. Mandle & Co., a small packaging and brand design firm in Paramus, New Jersey, I was forced to convert to digital thinking in 1985, a year after the Macintosh

computer premiered. There I was fortunate to be a pioneer in experimenting with Adobe Illustrator and QuarkXPress, in those days where the idea of a color printer was as unheard of as a stat camera is today.

Of course, designers are more likely to be digital boomers as well as artists now, as technology is part of all facets of our daily lives, but just because one grew up with the tools does not make one an artist. It can sometimes be dangerous to have a digital boomer in charge of design. The digi-boomer may have been promoted because they chose a design career as a result of technology-enhanced skills, and not talent. It might sound mean, but these people can be prevalent in big business. The problem is that usually only the talented creatives notice, but sadly the entire organization suffers.

Imagine the power they have. These creative leaders hire the talent, are responsible for growing and evaluating them, and set the vision for the entire company. (Or, at least, they should.)

One reason why there are so many under-qualified evaluators in business is because of

p.136 >> *Left:* CD cover design for a compilation of music featured at The Big Chill festival, and distributed by Resist Records. Design by Vault 49. *Right:* The pixelated graphics on designer Molly Regan's album design for Michael Hoska mirror the album's electro breaks and house synth pop. p.137 >> *Top left:* Valerie Ormiston pairs her silk-screen graphics in stylish colors with quality rag papers and

wood in her Vermont-based company, Pikku, which produces wallpaper, fabric and stationery goods. "Pods" wrapping paper by Pikku. *Top right:* "Crazy Daisy" pattern by Pikku. *Bottom:* "Loopi" pattern by Pikku.

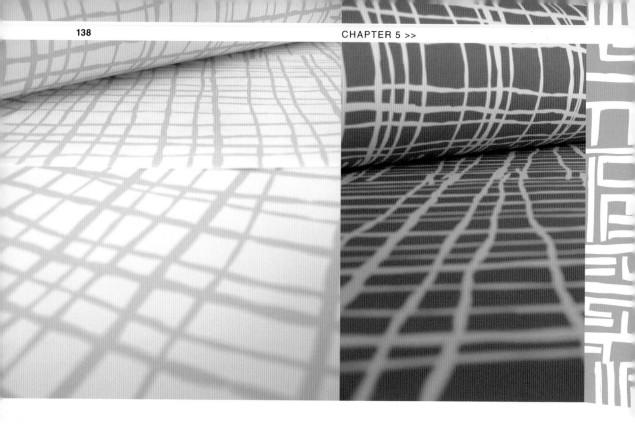

the long gap before technology was adopted but after many designers were hired. At the time, few designers bothered to learn the new skills of creating art on a computer, leaving a gap for more technically proficient creatives to take over. These "production minded" individuals had once been relegated to the back rooms of the art department, where their accuracy and ability to draw neat, straight lines meant they faced a future of paste-up and inking. Remember, these were the days of two art departments, technical and creative. Commercial art was a trade. For decades, design professions required both

right-brain and left-brain thinkers. Whatever made us believe that things had changed? We all want to believe that we can master both, but few ever do.

The ones who adopted technology early have not necessarily used the tools to the best effect. I wager that a connection can be made between those early adopters of design technology and the current state of creative misdirection that exists in corporate creative groups, and the new generation of brilliant creative work that is emerging from independent artists and designers. It's not necessarily

p.138 >> *Left:* "Screen Door Blu" pattern by Pikku. *Right:* "Screen Door Carrot" pattern by Pikku. p.139 >> "Amaze" pattern by New York City pattern designer Julia Rothman.

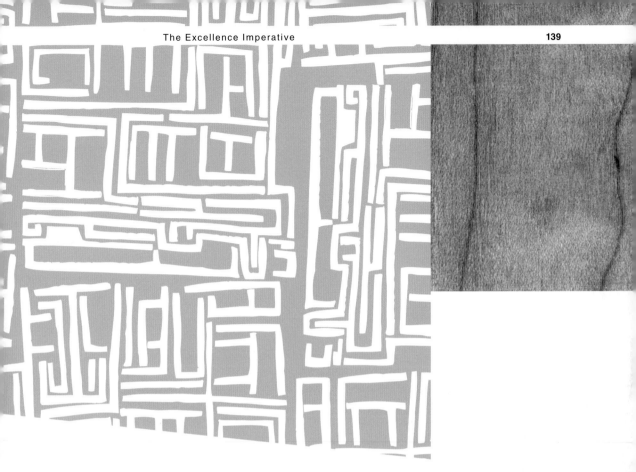

an age issue at all, for many older creatives who avoided using early digital tools are now transitioning with no ill effects and producing equally stunning work as those talented folks who have been using the tools for years.

In the future, historians may look back and see this effect more clearly. From my personal perspective, I can identify numerous peers who adopted tools early, some successfully and others not so successfully, and other peers who avoided the transition to technology until later in their careers and eventually found that the newer tools allowed greater creativity.

Either way, the twenty-year period between early desktop publishing and now did not turn out to be a significant period of aesthetic transition. Early on, there were fears that it would destroy design with dangerously skewed type and deconstructed galleys in magazine layouts, but nothing really happened other than a slowing-down of visual progress while we became caught up with stepped gradations and the limits of 256 colors. Digital design has caught up to the industry standards, and we are now seeing amazing talents from young designers who grew up with technology. Instead of the

designers who embraced technology early, getting a leg up on new designs, this "digital boomer effect" resulted in a generation of visual leaders who perhaps would have been more efficient on the boards than defining style and choosing from a color palette window. Worse yet, they are the ones evaluating the other designers. Thankfully, the newer generation of designers who were raised with the computer see no difference between their ideas and their tools. So the shift has begun from reinterpreting design to a digital palette, to one where the two are integrated.

A new generation of designer/creatives with the luxury of immense resources and who are free to assemble information and combine influences is leading to amazing new expressions. The future is suddenly starting to look bright again.

But we must proceed carefully. Right now we are at a dangerous tipping point. Those in charge of design direction are setting a direction based not on actual movements or influences, but on a skewed perspective of what they themselves deem appropriate. There is also a younger generation of tal-

p.140 >> *Left:* "Native" pattern by Julia Rothman. *Right:* "Cameras" pattern by Julia Rothman. **p.141** >> "Wheels" pattern by Julia Rothman.

ent eager to deliver solutions but whom are unclear on what the actual problems are and who have no idea how to filter, digest and use the information presented to them as influence. The future of design is in sight, but the ones who will reach it first will be either those who are independent or those who have the insight and vision to make sweeping changes to their creative groups. Only then will the balance shift to a model where knowledgeable and talented leaders actually lead, direct and inspire teams with the same mindset.

Knowledge Is Essential

I keep returning to the idea of education for a reason. Knowledge is the key, and design deficiency has a direct correlation to deficiency in knowledge. You must know what influences design, including art and design history, who the creative peers of today are, and who is being recognized for leading the pack.

The most successful leaders of any area of expertise know who got there first, who pioneered practices and who made significant contributions. Jockeys know who rode in what race, when, and who won. Architects know Frank Lloyd Wright's contributions to modern architecture, including his successes and failures. Artists know which movement they relate to, and why Jackson Pollock's work is important and not just splashes of dripped paint that a five-year-old can do. Take any profession, even a non-creative one like medical doctor, horticulturist, dog breeder or beekeeper. People in these professions are experts; they can explain every facet of the profession. They might subscribe to journals about their profession, attend seminars, or even have a bumper sticker that says, "Caution—Beekeeper on Board."

Then, why is it that so many of today's creatives, both leaders and designers, don't share the same passion in design as others do in their chosen expertise? Find out who your design leader's design hero is. Who is their current favorite designer? Favorite architect? What magazines do they subscribe to? It all comes down to passion. I am continually shocked when I speak at design conferences and ask what interests people have, and all I get are a few hands raised. I have evaluated creative teams where no one had a subscription to a design magazine—and they were all designers! I even had photographers in a corporate

p.142, p.143 >> "Bavaria" pattern by Julia Rothman.

photo studio who could not name a photographer they admired, nor the title of a photography magazine or organization, but, in the next breath, exclaim, "How dare you state that I don't have any passion?" I'm sorry, but even if you are exhibiting your work in a museum and traveling the globe, authentic work comes from the context you assemble, and context must be built from knowledge that is fed by passion.

Design as a Trade

Manufactured design is even advertised as a trade on late-night television. You've probably seen the commercials for local trade schools and colleges: "Learn a trade that can make you money." Then they list web design, HTML, Adobe Photoshop, and other design tools that you can learn in a few quick courses—the same way you can become a nail technician or an auto mechanic. No, no, no!

Design is not beauty school; it's a lifestyle.

In a time when billions of dollars are spent building brands that must have meaning to the consumer, the sooner we all realize the difference that real talent brings, the better the chance that innovation will stop being a buzzword, and become an actual result.

When you really think about it, many of today's business buzzwords are from the lexicon of art and design. Words like "authenticity," "excellence," "meaning," "story," and "innovation"—all are the emotional reasons why any gifted artist or creative creates. The difference is that we rarely ever need to articulate why we create—it's just a natural process. It's why creatives laugh a little when they hear these words used as business logic, and why they sometimes regard those who begin using such buzzwords—when they never paid any attention to them before—with suspicion.

Creatives innovate not because their job asks them to, but because they cannot help it. It's what they do. They would be innovating wherever they were. That might be the real reason that Google, Nike and Apple are at the top of the innovation mountain. They don't know any better. No one told them that they couldn't innovate. It's the same with small design firms that suddenly find that their natural proficiency in innovation landed them a huge client (most likely Coca-Cola, Nike or another trend-savvy corporation that recognizes the opportunity before others do). That's something small visionary designers

p.144 >> "Hand Tile" is proof that almost anything can become a pattern. Pattern by New York designer Julia Rothman. **p.145 >>** Batman Year 100 logo design by Rinzen for *Batman Year 100* comic series.

p.146 >> *Top:* Animal designs by Australian design firm Rinzen for credit cards for Cornerbank, a Swiss bank. *Bottom:* Design for Heavy Trash album, *Heavy Trash*, by Rinzen. **p.147** >> *Discover Ram* by L.A. artist and designer Steven Harrington.

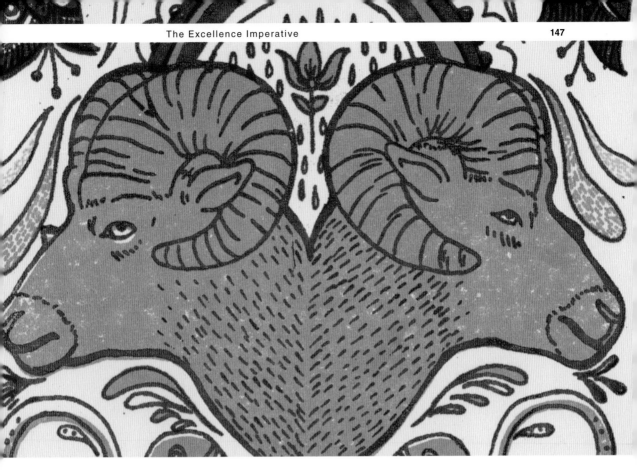

and start-up creative groups share: the same giant clients who "get it."

That is also why mature businesses continually struggle with the whole "innovation" challenge. Traditional businesses, especially those well established, grow a different culture of creativity, one fed by strategy and process, not by vision or design excellence.

CREATIVE LEADERSHIP

As the bar is raised on design, changes in both creative leadership and creative strategy will undoubtedly occur. Business and commerce depend on this change, and so does culture. In the future, brands are as likely to become meaningful cultural icons as design pillars are. With this will come the need for real visual management, not just textbook strategy. The whole idea of strategy and design has been flipped upside down by the Internet and by globalization, and perhaps even more so by environmental shifts in thinking.

Traditional models such as brand extensions and packaging are less important as the industry becomes more concerned with sustainability and less focused on big-brand thinking

and annual line-look upgrades. Frito-Lay, for instance, recently changed its snack packaging to appear less-designed and more environmentally friendly. The focus is instead on how a brand contributes to one's lifestyle—in other words, how it brings meaning.

Making Changes to a Creative Organization

The best place to make significant changes is not with your design team, but with who is directing and hiring them. Start at the top. The evaluator. The creative directors and heads of design decide, or at least influence, the creative team's direction, so it is important to have leaders who are on the same page of design.

The reason for a lack of innovation is rarely a lack of talent; it is most likely the fault of the evaluator. Nothing is more dangerous to design execution than self-validation. In the past, art departments have been protected from the suits in sales and marketing interfering in design. Now, more than just the creative directors evaluate art design: it can be the head of marketing, director of sales, CEOs, the spouses of CEOs. This evaluation

p.148 >> *Discover Owl* by Steven Harrington. **p.149** >> Room design for Hotel Fox in Copenhagen by Australian design firm Rinzen.

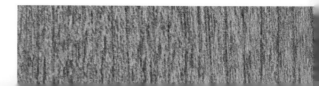

holds a lot of power. It can make or break a design by claiming it "not cool" or "right on trend." Too many cooks are evaluating the soup, and any one of them can say "make it pink," "green doesn't sell," or "I like this or that," all of which results in scribbled notes and directives beamed to their design staff's BlackBerries. "He hates green, make it pink, don't ask why"—probably because no one bothered to ask why.

As design becomes more unpredictable, it is as easy for someone to say he can evaluate design as it to claim he is a designer. This dan-gerous trio—faux designer, faux evaluator and faux validator—has resulted in a system that needs significant adjustment. This shift must result in authentic talent being recognized and rewarded for their gifts, which should then lead to innovation. True inspiration will then be allowed to rise to the top without bias or fear. This will help eliminate the need for justification against existing models or proven formulas, and will open the door for potential innovation that doesn't measure itself again old rules that limit. Who needs trends if you have the endless power of the creative mind to rely on again?

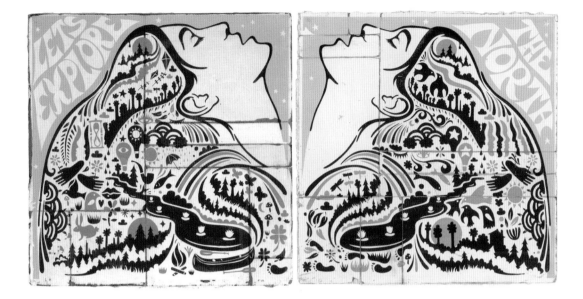

Just as curators are responsible for a museum exhibition, the evaluator of design is ultimately responsible for the outcome. They hold the power to change, to guide and to inspire those who are inspirable (for not everyone is inspirable). Evaluators are the key to change.

Design Leaders Oversee, Not Direct

The most effective curators posses not just the necessary business skills to manage, but most critically, they must have a visual intellect that directs their choices. If they have a highly developed language in design that can communicate with both the artists and the clients, all the better. Most importantly, curators manage visual direction, and since they are knowledgeable and informed, they earn the trust and admiration from their artists. This cycle of respect and nurturing allows for strong visual development that affects culture in profound ways. It's easy to see why the most successful creative leaders behave more like curators than creative directors. Pairing lead culture curators with leading experts in talent can only result in highly innovative product. This is the model of the most innovative companies that come to mind—Apple, Nike, and Disney.

p.150 >> *Discover Bear* by Steven Harrington. p.151 >> *Both the North* by Steven Harrington.

As curators, evaluators of creative talent have more power to steer thinking and expression—sometimes even more than the artist has.

Hiring Talent

Design may come from designers, but it starts with the creative leader. Generally, the best creative people are also super-smart and want to solve problems by themselves. They continually strive to win, but they are not afraid to fail. Managers sometimes see these traits as problematic. It is much easier to build a creative team with individuals who fit a more desirable mold—conformists and linear-thinking staff members who may be easier to manage, but less likely to create real innovation. The unpredictability of moody talent frightens managers, who demand consistent results. And it is these same creative leaders who will scare off the highly talented people. Balance is required, of course. After all, you do eventually have to release your design so it can be printed. But in the "let's innovate" future all of business is calling for, managers who serve their company by favoring the dependable deliverers over the feisty futurists will be doing

p.152 >> *Discover Rabbit* by Steven Harrington. **p.153** >> *Ship in a Bottle*, a Death Cab for Cutie poster by Steven Harrington.

* THE NAKED COWBOY DIDN'T REALLY SHOUT THIS, BUT PERHAPS IF HE → BANNERS (INSTEAD OF STANDING AROUND POSING FOR TOURISTS IN HIS UNDERPANTS), SPENT SOME TIME WANDERING AROUND LOOKING AT ALL OF THE HE WOULD. OH AND, WHERE I COME FROM, ONE IS NOT OFFICIALLY NAKED IF ONE STILL HAS ONE'S UNDERPANTS ON.

themselves, their company and the world of design a great disservice.

To management, the solution is simple. If you are in the position of demanding talent, then hire talent. If you are having problems attracting talent, look to your evaluators, for the change may need to begin there. If your product needs to be a breakthrough, then hire the most visually talented design leaders that you can afford, since that is where the talent originates. Talent and culture creation is where innovation starts. And in the end, innovation and originality in our overdesigned world has become the most effective way to compete in the "sea of sameness" that is evolving before our eyes.

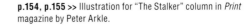

p.154, p.155 >> Illustration for "The Stalker" column in *Print* magazine by Peter Arkle.

Be ORIGINAL

1

CULTURE CREATORS ARE ORIGINAL

Culture creators don't follow established leaders. Their ultimate goal is originality—something that is often difficult to identify until they find it. It is generally a moving target that they are trying to get in their sight.

Culture creators are generally acutely aware of their position and status in the greater scheme of world cultural development. Their vision is often so clear to themselves that they have little patience with those who fail to connect intellectually to their unconventional processes.

Since boldly going where no one has gone before is often a scary proposition for most people, culture creators can be perceived as arrogant by some. In a world steeped in the familiar, originality can be frightening.

Culture creators never default to a formula. They prefer to sow the seeds of phenomenon.

CULTURE CREATOR »

2

CULTURE CREATORS ARE INTERESTED IN VALIDITY

Culture creators listen to their inner voice above anyone else's. They may be blind to the importance of their own contribution to world culture, and they believe that culture growth is a phenomenon, not predetermined.

Not motivated by pleasing their bosses or their company, they are instead focused on how the end-user desires what they produce.

They are usually good at assessing the capabilities of someone who is evaluating them. Therefore, they resent evaluation and critique unless it comes from a validator whom they deeply respect—preferably another cultural leader.

Truth is of the utmost importance to culture creators.

BE *Real*

Be Curious

CULTURE CREATORS HAVE ENDLESS CURIOSITY

Culture creators are insatiably curious and constantly learning. Culture creators demand high stimulation of all the senses.

Obsessed with "things," these are the people who find wonder in collecting unusual or discarded ephemera—the type treatments of vintage sales brochures, color palettes from mid-century modern books, certain colors of pottery glazes from the 1920s.

They spend any spare time cruising the Internet, discovering new things. They often have multiple interests and hobbies: gardening, surfing, raising canaries, breeding show dogs, sewing plush animals, cooking jams and jellies, collecting and reupholstering 1960s furniture. They assemble massive collections of books, travel to exotic locations and sometimes find the idea of relaxing horrifying. Boredom is rarely tolerated.

CULTURE CREATOR >>
4

CULTURE CREATORS RESPECT RARITY

Culture creators are obsessed with not only observing life, but with studying the debris of life. They place value on what others deem worthless, and they see wonder and find influence in the refuse of everyday life.

Culture creators celebrate rare expressions of individuality. They are attracted to original objects, either man-made or those ephemeral creations of nature. They have a unique perspective on life and often craft their own identities from a complex mixture of categorizing, cataloging and collecting.

Something that is one-of-a-kind may be priceless to a culture creator.

5

CULTURE CREATORS DEVELOP THEIR INTELLECT

Much like a terrier on a scent, the mind of a culture creator is wired to learn, learn, learn. They have an enormous respect for the history of art and design. Every past movement, every zeitgeist creative leader, every cultural icon in the design world, they know and celebrate.

Understanding things such as why the opulence of Victorian style affected the Arts and Crafts movements's stark purity is just the sort of fact retention that moves a culture creator to learn even more. Culture creators can identify nuances in influence and have an insatiable appetite for knowledge that can affect their creative work. They use knowledge as a building tool that allows them to establish context and relevance into every idea they invent.

BE Smart

CULTURE CREATORS CREATE FEARLESSLY

Be FEARLESS

Culture creators are fearless. They are naturally tactical and strategic, though not necessarily in the business sense of the terms. They seek challenges, such as attempting to solve unthinkable problems.

They surround themselves with peers of equal or greater significance. If challenges are set too low for them, there are generally bad results.

On the other hand, high challenges paired with highly-skilled creators often result in extraordinary work.

Achievement and success for the fearless might mean changing conventions or even establishing new ones. These fearless leaders boldly go where others have only dreamed.

Be THE EXPERT

CULTURE CREATORS DEVELOP EXPERTISE

Nothing ticks off a culture creator more than incompetence. Culture creators have little tolerance for underperformers, poseurs, fakers, dishonest designers or opinions from unqualified evaluators. They may be perceived as naive or even arrogant, since their ideas and recommendations are often based on where culture has directed the project and not the solution that meets the client perspective.

Becoming an expert in their niche or talent is more important to them than pleasing the client or their boss, so conflicts can easily arise. Culture creators respect proven expertise in most any field, and real achievement is measured more through the quality and efficacy of what one has created rather than by its mass appeal or commercial potential.

CULTURE CREATOR »

8

CULTURE CREATORS ARE ATTRACTED TO EXCELLENCE

Culture creators have a deep passion for excellence in design as well as other disciplines. Excellent food, music and film are inspiring to them. They have a true appreciation for things that are done with skill and attention to detail, whether it is perfect stitching in a shirt, an intriguing set design or a perfectly composed gourmet meal.

Just as they prize knowledge, originality and expertise, culture creators are attracted to a job well done. An amazing attention to detail, an exceptionally well-thought-out concept, or a stunning execution will get their attention. Better yet, a truly excellent creation will have all these qualities.

Be OBSESSIVE

CULTURE CREATORS ARE RESEARCHERS

Culture creators are obsessed with research. They are more likely to invest time in informing themselves with exhaustive research before assembling solutions, a practice which is sometimes misdiagnosed as procrastination.

They may have an advantage over the more process-driven problem solvers who are more likely to default to a less informed solution or a systematic approach rather than a radical culture-changing vision. The culture creator is driven to fully understand all the possible dynamics that could factor into a solution before establishing any attempts at assembling innovative strategies.

Where many novice creatives jump ahead to find a solution to a challenge, culture creators first invest time in thorough and informed research. They assess the challenge and its context in order to fully understand all the dynamics that could factor into a solution before establishing innovative strategies.

CULTURE CREATOR »
10

CULTURE CREATORS ARE RESPECTFUL

Be conscious

Have you ever had to go on a diet to lose a few pounds? One of the basic tenets all successful diets share is the idea of "practicing conscious eating." Practicing conscious creativity means that you consider every influence, you taste each bite. Culture creators exercise mindful creation all the time because it all connects for them. Their ideas flow from a sea of influence which has been collected over years, and analyzed, evaluated and sometimes reconsidered before being stored away in their brains.

Culture creators respect the history of design, as well as the future. They build context and relevance into every solution they create.

Remember, the human intellect is full of pre-recorded information, ideas that have come from other minds. It has all been thought through, considered, digested, strategized. At the same time, an entire army of people have formed perceptions based on what they have experienced. A certain amount of respect is due to those who have come before.

>>> *CHAPTER*

CONSCIOUSLY
CREATING

Why bother designing anything if everything is already designed?

A good question—if the premise is true, however. Is everything already designed? Is there nothing else that can possibly be new?

Some of you might think it's true, that today's design is formulaic. One can revisit the past, combine various random influences, pay homage or simply present volumes of visual solutions, and then let the clients choose what they like best. Others may feel the complete opposite, that there has never been a time when so many resources have been available. A virtual world library is available at the click of a mouse. Now we can assemble, search, explore and collect specific research that can lead to new and exciting solutions. There may never have been a better time to be a designer.

Two completely different views. So, which is right?

The answer lies in our brains, the gray matter that both haunts and inspires each of us. The way we think and process information, that which makes us each individuals, is the key to visual innovation. In order to master creating,

p.167 >> *Top:* Industrial Canvas Trash Coal Bag for the Jack Spade line by designer Abby Clawson Low. *Bottom:* An innovative wall mural by artists/designers Patrick Corrigan and Karen Gelardi, who designed and painted this piece in their home in Portland, Maine. The image was featured on the popular design blog Design*Sponge. Today, creative expression can be shared globally and instantly.

you must master how to use your mind effectively. This means learning to listen to your thoughts, evaluate and process everything you see, analyze and restructure, and then file it away for future reference. In order to harness creativity, you, as a creative, must act on what you see. It is no longer enough to just see and experience more than others, since everyone on the planet is seeing and experiencing more and more. What makes you different is how you process everything that your eyes see, and we all evaluate and process differently.

THE CREATIVE MIND

Processing information effectively requires constant education and training. Otherwise, we never grow or change our perspective and we end up evaluating everything against what we have established as acceptable criteria. We all are guilty of this, so it is essential that we update our education. We have all been at presentations where the responses are, "I don't like green," or "I don't like the pointy shapes, but I like the oval ones." Subjective responses are shallow and generally uninformed. Teaching your mind to evaluate against a set of

p.168, p.169 >> Providence, Rhode Island, designer Molly Regan's greatest challenge was to create a holiday poster that was modern without referencing a specific religious holiday. The result is this Jingleball poster for Boston's Kiss 108 FM.

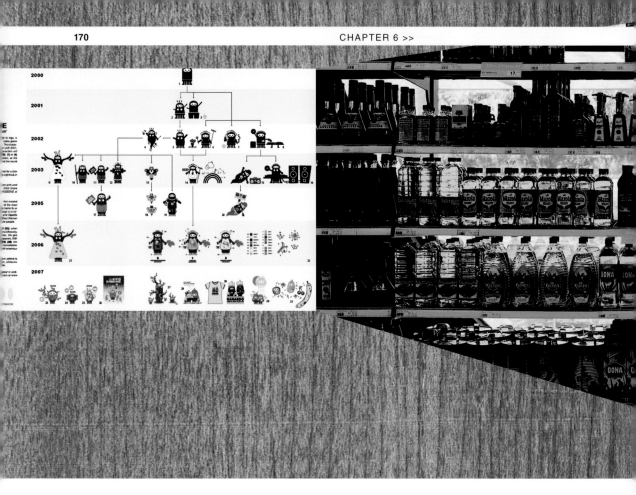

constantly updated criteria will allow you to respond objectively and provide a conscious awareness of what informed your solutions.

Creative minds are both a gift and a burden, as any designer knows. Many creatives struggle with focus and procrastination, yet scientists are finding that what may appear as quirks or dysfunction is actually part of the process of designing. Procrastination may simply be nature's way of sending a message that we need more time to effectively analyze the problem. Waiting to the last minute sometimes means that you had the opportu-

nity to gather even more information, and the simple act of choosing the right influence has resulted in a more brilliant solution since you had more analysis to choose from. Procrastination may actually be an important part of the process.

John Maeda, a graphic designer at the MIT Media Laboratory, says that procrastination may actually be necessary in some cases. He makes his point on an entry on his blog, SIMPLICITY (http://weblogs.media.mit.edu/SIMPLICITY/), where he posits that many creatives tend to overcommit to creative projects.

---

p.170 >> *Left:* Family tree for a fictional character by artist and designer Kanardo. *Right:* MPreis, Austria's stylish grocery chain. Photo © 2007 Lucas Schaller. **p.171 >>** *Top:* Vintage Ray Patin advertising still. *Bottom:* Windowseat Lounge chair by Mike and Maaike.

This reduces the amount of time they now have for their personal creative projects, leaving them with the feeling that they've sold their creative soul (i.e., creative personal time), and now have no time left to "squander away for the heck of it."

Maeda's theory takes an interesting turn, though, when he suggests that at the very moment of extreme procrastination, one of those moments that drives your clients crazy, when every second becomes exceedingly costly and you hate being a designer, creativity emerges. Maeda theorizes that it is in these "impossible moments that miracles tend to happen." He calls it "necessary procrastination."

Design and Science

New perspectives on creativity are coming from, of all places, science. Evolutionary psychologists, such as the University of New Mexico's Geoffrey Miller, are studying creativity and the connections creative people make between related and unrelated domains. Call it insight or inspiration, science is shedding new light on the mysteries of the creative brain, and discovering that those

p.172 >> Summerjam is Germany's biggest reggae festival. Poster design by Molly Regan/Logica Design.

"ah-ha" moments that we all occasionally have are not accidents at all, but are the result of a complex response that may be rooted deep in our psyche.

Miller makes a connection between Darwin's theories of sexual selection, how animals choose their mates based on appearance. Designers may share an aesthetic experience that is wired in us by Mother Nature herself. Darwin noted that mammals, birds, reptiles and fish have the aesthetic taste to prefer some partners to others. This is why in the world of nature we see an array of sexual ornaments such as decorative peacock tails, pink bare baboon butts and emerald dung beetles. Flowers even attract pollinating insects through aesthetic attraction. We cannot dismiss the natural phenomenon of humans as very visual art makers.

As cognitive psychologists study human creativity, many are still confounded by the great mysteries of the human experience—such as imagination and art expression—and the limits or limitless scope of defining the human experience in words. Some even concede that it may be artists and creative people who

p.174 >> *Top left:* Vintage Bab-O Cleanser packaging. *Top right:* Vintage Glad Straws packaging. *Bottom:* Skate deck design by Andrew Groves of IMAKETHINGS. *Background:* Kiss concert poster design by Molly Regan of Logica Design, Providence, Rhode Island.
p.175 >> *Right:* Album design for Txoka Txoka by Molly Regan, Logica Design.

remain fearless in addressing human nature. Regardless, science is telling us that our gift of design may indeed be magic, since even science can't explain why some are better at it than others. It is no wonder why business professionals struggle with how to fit the creative individual into the highly structured world of linear processes, delivery dates and realistic deadlines. It's also why those creatives who end up being successful in business tend to be those who are less innovative but more effective at delivering against a linear process. Perhaps this should be a consideration when businesses begin to evaluate why their

creativity production isn't as competitive as it once was.

Desire for Stimulation

The human desire for identity and significance is growing stronger and taking different paths all the time, as the recent rise in religion proves. And the same can be said for the human need for self-expression. The very fact that we all enjoy creating speaks to what may be a very primal need to make things. As our world grows more modern, we have lost so much of our connectivity with purpose.

p.176 >> Summerjam poster by Molly Regan, Logica Design. **p.177 >>** *Top:* Goodie Goodie logo by Rinzen of Australia. *Bottom:* Black Stone Stool by Marcel Wanders.

The global blur toward sameness threatens to cause us to lose our identity.

It's so hard to be different today that it's no wonder that the recent rise in do-it-yourself stores and self-expression are appealing. Where else can we express ourselves in real life? One of the greatest benefits of living in a modern world is that we have both the luxury of more free time and the ability to create, even if we are not creative. But humans are creative, naturally curious and inclined to create.

Zoologists say that many species demand stimulation or they will not thrive. Imagine

if humans were kept in a zoo. What would it take for them to be happy? What environment would be necessary? Some might simply need a cooler of beer, a reclining chair and a house trailer, but most humans with a high intellect would require so much stimulation and so many tasks that no zoo could ever keep up with the demand. It's probably why humans don't make good pets!

The thing that defines humans from the rest of the animal kingdom is our minds. The simple fact that we can use tools and create makes us so unique that the only species that come close are chimpanzees and Darwin's finches, and even then, we are talking about one mastering the pounding of a rock to open a nut, and the other using a thorn to extract a juicy grub from an acacia branch. Hardly comes close to designing a 110-story glass and titanium skyscraper, does it?

Not that we all need to design skyscrapers to meet our need for creativity, but human life thrives with as much creative expression as it has time for. The recently acquired ability to mix one's own music or edit a movie on a laptop and post it for the world to share is

p.178 >> Coca-Cola Light Plus bottle designed by San Francisco design firm Office. p.179 >> 2006 Office holiday card design.

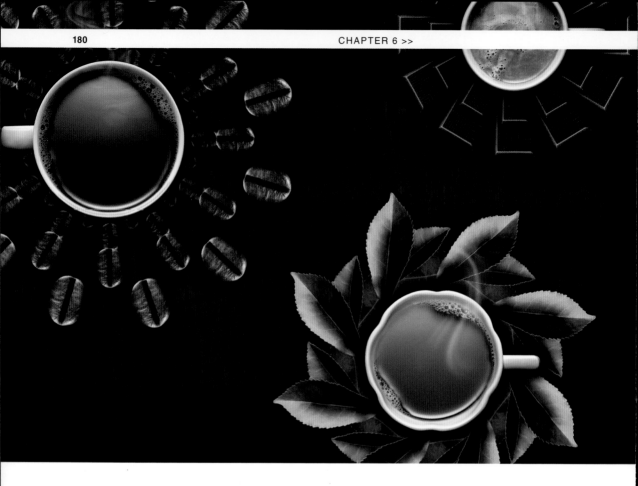

true proof that the human ability to create has not been lost. One may even argue that we are just beginning a phase of amazing creative potential as technology becomes more advanced and affordable and allows for more free time and expression.

THE BEGINNING
OF THE CREATIVE AGE

We are at the beginning of an age where visionary is king. You are in charge of the future of culture—not the marketer, not the sales force and not the retailer. Ultimately, it is you, the creative. Creativity has earned a respect in our culture that has elevated creatives from the dark and isolated art departments to designed environments with natural lighting and flexible hours. As businesses learn to give creatives whatever they want, they are also seeing a new trend—creatives leaving to work independently. Creatives can now work from wherever in the world they wish: a ski lodge, a beach house, or a New York City loft. Boundaries are disappearing for those creatives who are able to deliver their magic product to a world hungry for visual excellence. Our digital world

p.180, p.181 >> Chaqwa campaign designs by Office. © 2007 The Coca-Cola Company. **p.181** >> *Bottom left:* Flos Zeppelin lamp design by Marcel Wanders. *Bottom right:* Chaqwa campaign designs by Office. © 2007 The Coca-Cola Company.

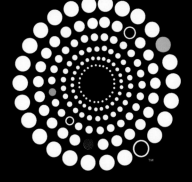

now connects client with artists with a click and a cable.

Designers are even reaching the boardrooms of the world's biggest corporations. Company after company elevates their most visually articulate to new lead positions that allow them to direct the appearance of product and design from newly invented roles we never could have dreamed of even ten years ago. Casting lead positions like chief creative officer and visual strategist has become a necessary move for savvy competitive companies that realize the value design brings.

It's Time to Fight for Honest Design

Stand up, designers—it's time to go to the mat for design excellence. This *is* a great time to be a designer, but in a world where anyone can design, you need to work harder in order to stand out. The best news is that you have a real weapon that cannot be imitated—passion. Passion defines an authentic designer from anyone who designs simply because it's fun, or just to have a career. Whether you agree or not, design is an art form. The best designers are first and foremost artists. Everything else can be learned. Honest design requires

p.182 >> *Top:* Moooi Boutique sofa by Marcel Wanders. *Left:* Marcel Wanders' designs for Lute Suites. *Center right:* Exterior of Lute Suites. *Bottom right:* View of interior of Lute Suites, designed by Marcel Wanders. **p.183 >>** *Right:* Staircase detail in Lute Suites, by Marcel Wanders.

talents that cannot be learned, only improved upon. Those gifts are passion, curiosity and drive. I firmly believe that without the art aspect, design is merely meaningless execution, not informed creation that moves people and changes the world.

Prepare yourself for a world of design professionals who don't all agree. While writing this book, I created an online poll on a professional networking site that asked the question: "What would you rather hire for your creative department—a tech genius, or a highly-talented and gifted artist?" I gave the restrictions that

respondents "could not answer with the obvious—both." The results surprised me. I had believed that the majority would see the obvious answer was the artist, the creative. But I knew I was in trouble when a friend called me up laughing. "I saw your post about artists versus technical designers," he said, "Did you see the responses? Everyone is *so* serious. Those people should really chill out!"

The next morning I checked my inbox, and I was actually a little shocked with how one-sided the responses were. Most of them said something to the effect of, "How dare you

p.184 >> Adidas Golf campaign. Photography by Office: Jason Schulte Design, San Francisco. **p.185 >>** Target's back-to-college campaign, "Independent Studies." Logo design and campaign imagery by Office: Jason Schulte Design.

INDEPENDENT STUDIES

confuse artists with designers," or, "How dare you say that technical wizards cannot be creative too." A surprising number of responses (15 of 47) said that they would rather hire the talented artist, but that I should be careful to not use the word "artist," since artists are not designers; artists are those who are driven by the "personal need to create."

Wow. My point exactly!

Creativity Is Unconventional

Designers (and all creative people, for that matter) have it tough. Independent thinking always runs against the grain of conventional processes. Even in these times of embracing creativity, it's still difficult to find total acceptance if your ideas are different. The most talented creatives will always be rare, a minority, and we all know how cultures treat minorities. People who do not fit in or are unconventional or different are seen as being "not normal." Conventional thinkers are so much easier to deal with. Being different is hard; it's no wonder so many designers end up trying to rationalize their solutions, even filtering them or dumbing them down, to make them more digestible in a white-bread business world.

p.186 >> Enviga packaging and design by Office: Jason Schulte Design. **p.187 >>** View of the Madagascar river channel from NASA's Terra satellite.

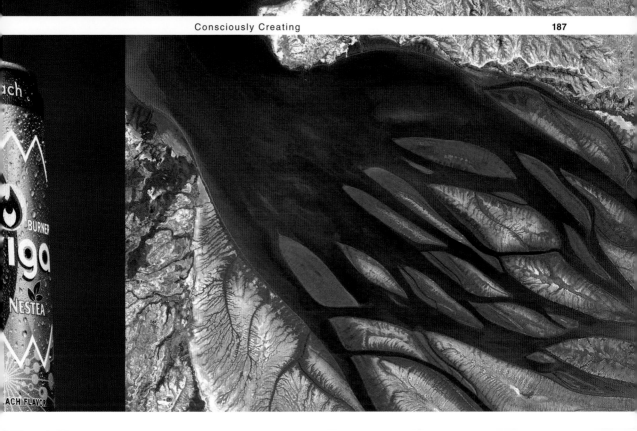

Overcoming the multitude of perceptions that exist about designers is paramount to accepting your talent and skills and confidently exercising what you do naturally. Strangely enough, the biggest abuser of this labeling is our own creative community, which turns on its own with such thinking. This is absurd, especially considering that business has begun to accept that design is valuable to the bottom line, and much more than a service. Think about all the cliché perceptions about creatives: They are all edgy, trendy, artsy, risk-taking, impractical, irresponsible, scatter-brained procrastinators with Attention Deficit Disorder who wear black, go against the norm, and don't listen or react well to criticism.

Why is it that so many creative peers turn on their talented brethren with such damaging posturing? One answer may be fear—a fear of inadequacy, or one that comes from deeply rooted conditioning resulting from decades of being told that we were all simply "creative services." The very unconventional nature of creatives is what helps inject value into designs. We need to accept that. It doesn't matter what our process is. The creative result is ultimately what matters.

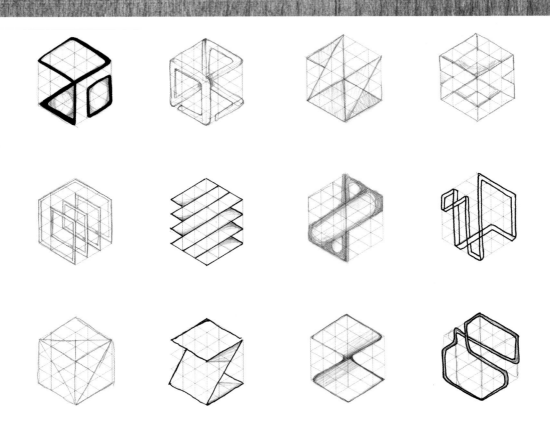

Getting It

"They just don't get it." How many times have we all said that? We feel that the world doesn't understand our work. All we designers have ever really wanted is to have everyone "get it." How easy it would be if everyone thought like a designer.

The reality is that most people don't. So, one of our jobs is to help people understand. But we cannot educate them until we first educate ourselves. We must be smarter. We must know what informs us, why it informs us and where this influence comes from. If you

can't do that, then how can you as a designer design? How can you problem solve, or create "new," or "get it" (and help others "get it") if you never did in the first place?

Here is where the divide begins. To "get it," not only must you understand, but you must be able to explain *why* you "get it" and where "it" comes from. Those with the capacity to share with those who don't understand "get it." They are the only ones who can save the future of design.

Designers have a job that goes far beyond discovering trends or blazing paths for new ones.

p.188 >> Concept sketches for Microsoft Zune logo and identity by Jager Di Paola Kemp Design (JDK) of Vermont. p.189 >> Zune packaging, advertising and logo design for Microsoft by JDK.

Today's designers must validate why their ideas are right. Gone are the days where one can simply sit behind a monitor and scroll through color palettes randomly selecting colors because they feel right. You must know why they feel right. Intuition is not a spirit inside you; it is fed by real exposure to content, and one must consume immense quantities of content to make an informed, intuitive decision. And guess what? Our modern environment is perfectly suited for intuitive creatives with talent. What artist would ever complain that there are too many colors to choose from, or too many materials? Those who feel overwhelmed are confused with the abundance of information, and decide that they can create without influence. They don't see the value of knowing which designer is "hot" or who won the Webbys. They think, "I don't need to pollute my mind with other people's idea of what is right," or, "I prefer to be original, not trendy." Such ignorance only breeds uninformed, blind designers.

I cannot stress enough the importance of education in art and design history. Equally as important, though, is study of the current design leaders. These contemporaries

p.190 >> Korbin Kameron wine ad by Office: Jason Schulte Design, Inc. p.191 >> *Inflorescence* by Tord Boontje.

are crafting original expressions in an over-designed world. How can anyone know what is original if he is unable to establish context? Others who create may isolate themselves because they simply do not understand what might be next, and find so much information out there that it is easy enough to create using familiar, pre-edited tools and palettes. More damaging is that these ideas are easier to sell to clients, since everything is already familiar and easier to understand. Unfortunately, "design excellence" is then defined by how accurate and cleanly executed a solution is, not by how innovative it is. In a digital world, where few can define difference, the only difference becomes the execution rather than the idea.

Whenever someone doesn't know how to evaluate design, they focus on how it was executed. As a designer, if you don't know how or why you arrived at a particular solution that you are recommending, you cannot deal with ambiguous responses such as, "Make it pop." Remember that you are pitching ideas and solutions to an uninformed audience. This will help you sell an honest, innovative idea.

p.192, p.193 >> Vintage Ray Patin stills courtesy of Amid Amidi/Cartoon Modern.

Courtesy of CWC International. www.cwc-i.com

Innovation is scary. Real innovation is new and different, and we all know how well different can go over. If you know how and why you arrived at your innovative solution, explaining your process will sell it. This will also prepare you for the inevitable responses that you'll get when you present a truly different and culture-changing idea. Having answers that address vague responses of people who don't know what to say will allow you to respond. Your answers will come from your influences. It is very difficult for anyone to argue with an authentic solution from a well-informed designer.

All design must be justified. Like any teacher, the designer must be knowledgeable in order to communicate accurate information both through the design solution and to the client. The most successful creatives know the history of design and of the world and how they factor into their design solutions. Only through knowledge can you defend your creation and define the process at which you arrived at the particular solution.

Design may be the best profession on earth. Come on, you get to create things! True designers range from highly talented creators who

p.194 >> *From left to right:* Illustration by Chico Hayasaki. *100 Girls* illustrations by Tina Berning. Illustration by Stina Persson. Illustration for *New York Times* editorial by Tina Berning. p.195 >> *From left to right: 100 Girls* illustrations by Tina Berning. Illustration by Stina

can influence as they invent, to geniuses who create culture. Because of the demand for design, any career path related to design is hotter than ever.

Design Is Like Sex …

Design is like sex. Dare I say it, sex as a service. Think about it …

It is personal, and different for everyone. The unspoken drive that moves one to design and create is an unconscious process with complex stimuli that we think about only at a very superficial level. In that sense, design is really

like a fetish. I know, weird. This is why design is such a mystery to non-creatives, and why evaluating anything creative in a business is "hands-off" to corporate human resource departments. It's too personal, too subjective and too messy.

Like sex, design is innate, yet it is partially a learned behavior from a complex set of factors that you learned on your own through experimentation or through exposure from peers. You internally processed these factors without advice or knowledge, since no one would ever explain it to you, and being left

alone allowed this to manifest itself in any way that pleased you. This ultimately defined your style.

In this way, your designs are uniquely you. Throughout your life, you hardly heard otherwise. In our culture, we rarely talk about what leads to design; it is just rewarded in superficial ways by our mothers and teachers, who never know how to evaluate it. Instead, they say, "Oh, honey, how beautiful. You are *so* talented!" and the six-legged doggy is stuck to the refrigerator, reinforcing at an early age that, "Hey, I must be good at this!" What adult would ever give negative feedback on something that was personal expression?

Think about other fields where talent plays a role, such as sports and music. As children, we knew our creative limits when we were picked last for the baseball team, or when the piano teacher tapped our fingers with a ruler as the metronome rhythmically ticked away. In visual arts, the feedback was always more vague, since no one ever comments critically on something as personal as imagination, especially when such skills cannot be measured by a test. No wonder so many

p.196 >> Today's animation community gets much of its inspiration from the high-style illustrations of Modernism's first wave in the 1950s and 1960s. Vintage advertising art is courtesy of Amid Amidi and published in *Cartoon Modern* (Chronicle Books). **p.197 >>** United Productions of America (UPA)/Amid Amidi/*Cartoon Modern*.

people struggle with design. At a time when individual performance and evaluation plays a critical role in our career paths, no one is equipped to understand design, much less evaluate or critique it.

Not only is the source of creativity a mystery, why we design is also not understood. Whatever drives the creative expression is so personal that we rarely admit it completely to ourselves. That keeps it a conundrum for others. But I doubt this will change. Keeping the analogy, imagine if sexual performance was to be evaluated in a boardroom. Most of

us would probably fail miserably, since we couldn't please everyone (not at one time, anyway). For whatever reason, we design. I'm okay with that. I really don't care why I design—I just need to.

One aspect of motivation that I struggle with is when other creatives say that they are "in a rut." They frequently ask me, "What can I do to get inspired?" Perhaps it is just me, but I never feel as if I am in a rut. I sometimes wonder if the problem is that it's not a rut at all, but maybe the problem is the road or the cart, or the horse pulling it. Nothing as small

p.198 >> Today's animation may feel retro to some people and new to others. The fact is, animators are looking to the past for inspiration. Vintage advertising still from Ray Patin Studios, now in the collection of Amid Amidi and published in *Cartoon Modern* (Chronicle Books). **p.199 >>** *Top:* Vintage Mr. Magoo animation still from UPA, courtesy of Amid Amidi/*Cartoon Modern. Bottom left:* Vintage animation still

from UPA. Courtesy of Amid Amidi/*Cartoon Modern*. *Bottom right:* Vintage advertising still from Ray Patin Studios, now in the collection of Amid Amidi/*Cartoon Modern*.

sublime.

confident.technics.

unswerving.attitude.

thastroj.rnudawakerin.nnse.drezign.

and insignificant as a rut should ever stop a driven creative. But ruts do happen. They come to those of us who are experiencing boring, unstimulating sameness that doesn't excite us. Being forced to create is actually the problem—more accurately, being forced to create on demand, on projects that we don't respect and find little stimulus from. Being in a rut is simply acknowledging that you are bored. Your job is unexciting. Creatives thrive on excitement and meaning. If you want your work to mean something and not be boring, a walk on the beach looking for inspiration is not going to do it. Making significant changes

to your life will. Since design is in our DNA, we need to accept our destiny, and begin to better define our designs so that others can see what we have to offer.

CONNECTIONS

For most of us, dream design projects are a fantasy. The daily grind of drive-through design and PowerPoint presentation backgrounds can get the best of us. Get out of your rut by virtually connecting with an outside community to share your work with. If you are an animator, create a blog and connect to other

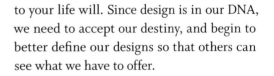

p.200 >> The composition in this poster by Karoly Kiralyfalvi shows how architectural styles are affecting graphic design principles. **p.201 >>** Sublime Trash logo by Karoly Kiralyfalvi.

animators with blogs. Compete in fun online challenges, or connect with studios and other animators through special interest groups on image sharing sites like Flickr. Most animators and graphic artists I know have deep and complex environments in Flickr and Blogger, where they share their image sets of esoteric themes that they might collect, such as vintage Mary Blair children's book illustrations or favorite cereals of the 1970s.

It is not uncommon for one animator's blog to be linked to a hundred other animators' blogs, including professionals at the massive anima-tion studios like Disney and Pixar or Cartoon Network. Young animators are also drawn to this virtual community, where they can share their projects and character sketches with the pros while still in school. They can receive informative feedback, valuable internships and even employment opportunities immediately upon graduating simply through connections within the animation design blog community.

Options and Opportunities

The most talented creatives in many fields of design have many opportunities. Martha

p.202 >> Deconstruction and abstraction can be seen in both architecture and in graphic design. Today, technology allows designers to deconstruct and reconstruct objects to make new forms and to redefine space and plane. A digital model by architect Zaha Hadid.
p.203 >> A poster by Karoly Kiralyfalvi.

Stewart Living Omnimedias hire dozens of creative interns annually. These must-have creative positions are awarded only after an extensive portfolio search. When a key creative position becomes available, the candidates have already been screened and are waiting. Talented designers may still be rare, but the digital connected world has made them easier to find. Consequently, these connections also make it easier for the talented to select which positions they want. They are actually finding their dream jobs, leaving employers and recruiters even hungrier for new talent than ever before.

The top talent has more options. They don't necessarily have to consider conventional jobs in corporations. They are more likely to work independently, or from home, or without an agent, and without the boundaries of the four cubicle walls. As young talented designers are recruited earlier and earlier by the global creative leaders, an equally talented population is deciding that making it on their own is not a pipe dream, but a reality. Web sites like Etsy and online creative communities like Coroflot, Behance, and LinkedIn make portfolios only a keyword search away from a planet of wealthy clients.

p.204, 205 >> Urban Outfitters founder Richard A. Hayne has transformed the once-abandoned Philadelphia Navy Shipyard into an inspiring space for creatives. This project's success lies with its broad creative team, including architect Jeffrey Scherer of MS&R, environmental experts, interior designers, and even documentation of the project's completion by architectural photographer Lara Swimmer.

Believe me, as an art buyer for a Fortune 500 creative company, it is increasingly difficult to find freelance talent who can produce game-changing designs and also have free time! The rare individuals with extreme visual talent who move trends forward find it hard to say no to work from the hot clients like Nike, Coca-Cola, Target and Hasbro. The reason these creatives are so in demand and all seem to share the same client list is that they are visual geniuses.

Which leaves the rest of the creative pack available. Not that they are not excellent

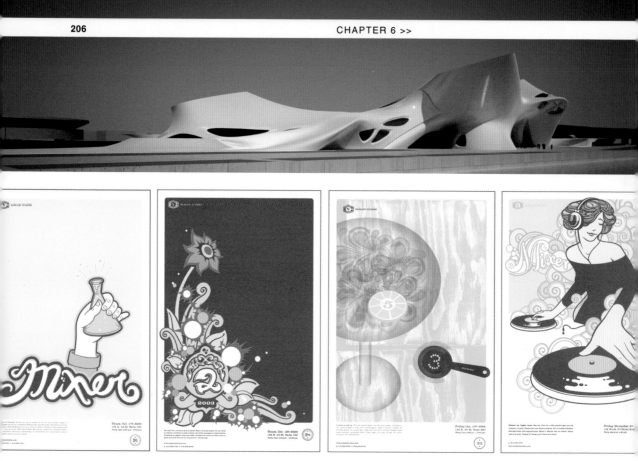

creatives, just perhaps not genius material. And let's face it, not everyone needs creative geniuses. Some businesses are not looking for market-moving visual solutions. (But shouldn't everyone demand "market-moving" solutions?)

If a tiny percent of the creatives in the world are these rare and brilliant (if not difficult!) geniuses, the majority is composed of designers with a wide range of skills and talents, gifted generalists who know a lot about a lot of things. But there is a third group that may have simply decided that design might be fun

or who are highly proficient with computer skills, but who also may have a role in design creation. The boundaries are all fuzzy, and depending on what expectations are set, there arguably is a creative job for everyone. But be careful here—such subjective definers as "doesn't get it" or "untalented" are hard to steer around if you cannot prove them, and the more intangible the evaluation is, the more inaccurate it risks being. Most creatives believe they are talented and artistic. The safest way to navigate these sensitive waters is with an evaluator that you trust. Remember to evaluate the evaluator first. As a capable

creative yourself, you too must factor in how you evaluate and integrate those who judge your work, just as you need to evaluate what informs your work.

Staying Ahead

Accepting modernity in whatever expression it arrives in is as important as understanding it yourself. It is far too easy to fall into the trap of not understanding a new style, and so dismissing it as irrelevant. This is a common and tragic mistake that many designers make as they move forward in their careers.

Not staying current with trends and styles, no matter what they evolve into, is as dishonest as not caring about what you are designing. I am not saying that everything must be modern, just that you must understand what modern design is at any moment in time to ensure that your work is being informed and positioned in an authentic way.

We all exist and function in a modern world. Practicing design requires that you know what aesthetic is appropriate and which is not. Realistically, most designers rarely, if ever, have the luxury to design truly culture-changing

p.206 >> *Top:* Zaha Hadid's concept for the Nuragic & Contemporary Art Museum in Cagliari, Italy, has many influences, but the foundational inspiration is biological: the sea. **p.206 >>** *Center:* Mixer invitations from Catalyst Studios. **p.207 >>** Detail of model by Zaha Hadid.

projects, but knowing where the edge of culture is at any moment means that your work is at least authentic, and has a place on the timeline of design. Know where you are right now, culturally, and target the future.

As creatives, the future may be more exciting than we could ever imagine. The opportunities are plentiful as technology progresses. Who could have ever predicted the positive outcome of design twenty years ago? Its role has been elevated to a place where suddenly we creatives seem to have dream jobs. One time, not so long ago, the highest position a creative could have in an organization would be that of Creative Director—but today, executive search firms are on the hunt for the next hot Futurist, Imagineer or Chief Creative Officer. Our culture has a heightened respect for design, and big business needs our brains. We cannot control where design is going, but we can be assured that the ride to get there will be exciting. It's up to us to create the world that is beyond trend.

p.208 >> *Top:* Today, we integrate multiple influences into our work. It's not uncommon to see vintage animation juxtaposed with digital typography or cut silhouettes on paper. This is a pattern Tord Boontje created for a Target Christmas promotion. *Center:* CD case for band Red Snapper by Non-Format of London. p.209 >> "Living In New York," a full page advertisement for Target by Melinda Beck.

PERMISSIONS

p.135 >> © 2004, Rinzen
p.135 >> © 2005, Rinzen
p.136 >> © 2005–2007, Vault 49
p.136 >> © 2007, Molly Regan
and Logica, Providence, RI
p.137 >> © 2007, PIKKU
p.138 >> © 2007, PIKKU
p.139 >> © 2007, Julia Rothman
p.140 >> © 2008, Julia Rothman
p.141 >> © 2008, Julia Rothman
p.142 >> © 2008, Julia Rothman
p.143 >> © 2008, Julia Rothman
p.144 >> © 2008, Julia Rothman
p.145 >> © 2007, DC Comics,
and Rinzen
p.146 >> © 2007, Rinzen
p.146 >> © 2005, Rinzen
p.147 >> © 2007, Steven
Harrington
p.148 >> © 2007, Steven
Harrington
p.149 >> © 2007, Rinzen
p.150 >> © 2007, Steven
Harrington
p.151 >> © 2007, Steven
Harrington
p.152 >> © 2007, Steven
Harrington
p.153 >> © 2007, Steven
Harrington
p.154 >> © 2007, Peter Arkle
p.155 >> © 2007, Peter Arkle
p.156–166 >> © Matt Mattus
p.167 >> © 2007, Kate Spade
p.167 >> © 2007, Patrick
Corrigan/Karen Gelardi

p.168 >> © 2007, Molly Regan,
Logica Design
p.169 >> © 2007, Molly Regan /
Logica Design
p.170 >> © 2007, Kanardo.
com//Unchi
p.170 >> Photo © 2007, Lucas
Schaller © 2007, MPreis
p.171 >> © 2007, Mike + Maaike
p.171 >> © 2007 Amid Amidi/
Ray Patin
p.172 >> © 2007, Molly Regan /
Logica Design, Providence, RI
p.173 >> © 2007, Molly Regan /
Logica Design, Providence, RI
p.174 >> © Molly Regan / Logica
Design, Providence, RI
p.174 >> © 2008, IMAKETHINGS
p.175 >> © Molly Regan / Logica
Design, Providence, RI
p.176 >> © Molly Regan / Logica
Design, Providence, RI
p.177 >> © 2007, Rinzen
p.177 >> © 2007, Marcel Wanders
p.178 >> © 2007 The Coca-Cola
Company
p.179 >> © 2006 Office:
Jason Schulte Design, Inc.
p.180 >> © 2007 The Coca-Cola
Company
p.181 >> © 2007 The Coca-Cola
Company
p.181 >> © 2007, Marcel Wanders
p.181 >> © 2007, The Coca-Cola
Company
p.182 >> © 2006, Marcel Wanders

p.183 >> © 2006, Marcel Wanders
p.184 >> © 2005 Taylor-Made
Adidas Golf
p.185 >> © 2006 Target Corporation
p.186 >> © 2006 The Coca-Cola
Company
p.187 >> NASA Image courtesy
of the US/Japan ASTER Science
Team, NASA/GSFC/METI/
ERSDAC/JAROS
p.188 >> © 2007, JDK
p.189 >> © 2007, JDK
p.190 >> © 2006 Office: Jason
Schulte Design, Inc.
p.191 >> © 2007 Studio
Tord Boontje
p.192 >> © 2007, Amid Amidi/
Cartoon Modern
p.193 >> © 2007, Amid Amidi/
Cartoon Modern
p.194 >> © 2007, CWC International Inc. All Rights Reserved.
http://www.cwc-i.com/
p.195 >> © 2007, CWC International Inc. All Rights Reserved.
http://www.cwc-i.com/
p.196 >> Vintage advertising art,
courtesy of Amid Amidi/Cartoon
Modern.
p.197 >> UPA/Amid Amidi from
Cartoon Modern.
p.198 >> Vintage Advertising
still from Ray Patin Studios,
now in the collection of
Amid Amidi/Cartoon Modern
(Chronicle Books).

p.199 >> Vintage animation
still from UPA. Courtesy of
Amid Amidi/Cartoon Modern
(Chronicle Books).
p.199 >> Vintage Mr. Magoo Animation still from UPA/courtesy
of Amid Amidi/Cartoon Modern.
p.199 >> Vintage Advertising
still from Ray Patin Studios,
now in the collection of
Amid Amidi/Cartoon Modern
(Chronicle Books).
p.200 >> © 2007, Karoly
Kiralyfalvi
p.201 >> © 2007 Karoly
Kiralyfalvi
p.202 >> © 2007, Zaha Hadid
Architects
p.203 >> © 2007 Karoly
Kiralyfalvi
p.204 >> © 2007, Lara Swimmer
Photography (www.swimmer-
photo.com)
p.205 >> © 2007, Lara Swimmer
Photography (www.swimmer-
photo.com)
p.206 >> © Zaha Hadid Architects
p.206 >> © Catalyst Studios
p.207 >> © Zaha Hadid Architects
p.208 >> © Tord Boontje, Target
p.208 >> © Non-Format
p.209 >> © Melinda Beck, Target

INDEX